*Marie,
Blessings!*

*Terry Burnside
(Revelation 4:11)*

RAPTURE READY

SEVEN GREAT AND TRUE FUTURE EVENTS

By Terry Burnside

www.xulonpress.com

ENDORSEMENTS

" "For The Lord Himself will descend from heaven with a shout, with the voice of an archangel, and with the trumpet of God. And the dead in Christ will rise first. THEN WE WHO ARE ALIVE AND REMAIN shall be "CAUGHT UP" (Raptured) together with them in the clouds to meet The Lord in the air. And we shall always be with The Lord. Therefore comfort one another with these words" (1 Thessalonians 4:16-18).

I imagine the author of this book would probably tell you that this passage is his favorite in all The Bible. The reason I can safely say this is that I know firsthand that Terry Burnside lives each day with what I would call a "Pauline" mentality and expectation. Let me explain what I mean by that statement. When Paul wrote I Thessalonians 4:17, he says "then 'WE' who remain alive," which means he really thinks he will be alive when the Rapture occurs. Terry lives every day of his life with the same enthusiastic expectation Paul did. Terry emphasizes the importance of everyone being *Rapture Ready*. I have known him for over 25 years. He is a soul winner for the Lord Jesus Christ and exhibits a deep sense of urgency that people should be ready for and expect Jesus to return at any moment. He really brings the Book of Revelation to light and explains salvation, all the signs, symbols, time tables, warnings, fulfilled prophecies, and prophecies yet to be fulfilled. The bottom line is this: there is not one Biblical prophecy left yet to be fulfilled before Jesus returns; it is just a matter of when the Father looks at Jesus and says, "Son, it's time to go pick up the kids!" When one reads *Rapture Ready*, they will be faced with a decision, "What are you going to do with Jesus?" Many of us remember playing hide and seek as kids, and Jesus is saying throughout the pages of Terry's book, "Ready or not, here I come!"

Rev. Sam D. Wiley
Pastoral Staff, Central Church
Collierville, Tennessee

In *Rapture Ready—Seven Great True Future Events,* Terry Burnside takes the reader on a thrilling and exciting futuristic journey from the Rapture of the Church to the Revelation of Jesus Christ (The Second Coming) to the final Restoration of all things. From a lifetime of study and teaching biblical prophecy, Burnside has ingeniously put together a scriptural end times time-line simple enough for the novice, yet intriguing for any student of eschatology.

In his own unique and direct style, Burnside passionately sets forth the Word of Truth by means of a clearly presented and soundly convincing Pre-tribulation and Pre-millennial position that commands serious reflection and review by all students of prophecy, regardless of their eschatological leaning. The reader learns early that the writer is a strong literalist. "If the literal sense makes good sense, seek no other sense." From that stance, Burnside freely and confidently argues, using Scripture to prove Scripture, his Pre-trib/Pre-mil theology on the soon return of Christ to gather His Bride from the four corners of the earth, snatching them from the seven years of tribulation coming upon the whole world, and taking them to the Marriage of the Lamb. The Rapture and the Millennium are fence posts to Burnside's book, and along with the reality of judgment and the lake of fire, he frequently urges his non-believing readers to come to faith in Christ while reminding believing readers to look up and long for the return of their King. The author's masterly grasp of God's eternal covenant with Israel and His loving and glorious plan for the Church are beautifully woven together throughout the book. Israel and the Church, brought together as one in Christ, enter the great timeless forever at the end of all things—which as Burnside cleverly depicts—is actually only the beginning!

Some will read this book once. Others will often return to it as they seek for themselves (and for those they love) to be *Rapture Ready*!

Rev. Gene Sauls
Pastoral Staff, Central Church
Collierville, Tennessee

Any maturing believer needs to grasp doctrine, heaven, and prophecy. There are plenty of books about doctrine, too few books on heaven, and a lack of books that one reads about prophecy. Prophecy immediately calls to mind the Books of Revelation or Daniel, seemingly esoteric descriptions of heaven and things to come, and our mind is boggled. It would take years to study the Scripture and then years to teach what the Scripture says on prophecy. Terry Burnside has done both studying and teaching. He has done the legwork and created a book that not only teaches Scripture, but puts prophecy in the proper context. He raises the simple question, "Are we ready for the Rapture?" Most of us like the idea and agree it will happen, but we surely don't have an apologetic base to support why we believe what we believe. Terry takes Scripture alongside Scripture to give us a general and a specific understanding of prophetic Scripture. There are times you are reading and the light comes on, connecting themes and illuminating Scripture in the most simple ways. Then you are taken on a journey as Terry pulls the threads together to make a case for Pre-tribulation and Pre-millennial eschatology. I enjoy Terry's style of writing that makes it easier to understand and fun to learn along the way. At the end of the book you must think for yourself and answer the question, "Am I ready for the Rapture?"

Rev. Don Gilbert
Chairman, Kingdom Community Builders
Memphis, Tennessee

DEDICATION

To my beloved family – my wife, Phyllis, and our children, Terri, Philip, Patrick, Taylor, and our two grandchildren, Hallie and Wyatt. Thank you for helping in ministry all these years. It is so true that when the husband/father/grandfather is in ministry, the whole family shares in ministry.

To my loving mother-in-law, Nell Cummings, who is the valuable age of 94. Her prayers have been felt and answered for many years.

To my dearest friends – Rev. Don Gilbert, Rev. Gene Sauls, and Rev. Sam Wiley.

Their trust and confidence over many years of companionship have blessed me above measure. They are faithful friends!

To my former pastorates in Forrest City, Arkansas, Good Hope Presbyterian Church and Ragland Memorial Presbyterian Church; in D'Lo, Mississippi, D'Lo United Methodist Church and Bethany United Methodist Church; in Houston, Mississippi, Faith Bible Church, and finally to Central Church in Collierville, Tennessee. God has given me great ministries. At Central Church, I learned the true philosophy of ministry is not only preaching and teaching. It is also ministering to the Body of Christ during life events such as births, deaths, hospitalizations, and extenuating circumstances. The Body of Christ is essential to ministry: "God…will not forget your work and the love you have shown him as you have helped his people and continue to help them" (Hebrews 6:10). Thank you Central Church!

To Steve and Judy Ashford who read and re-read the manuscript of *Rapture Ready* and greatly encouraged me during the process of writing. Steve is an Elder at Central Church. Judy is involved in women's ministries.

Finally, to Carol Wilemon who assisted me in editing *Rapture Ready*.

I'm so grateful for all of you.

ACKNOWLEDGMENTS

I attended Mid-South Bible College in the early seventies. For two years I had the privilege to be taught by Dr. James B. Crichton, for whom the school was later named. I sat on the front row in every class Dr. Crichton taught. He covered Prolegomena to Eschatology. I enjoyed Systematic Theology, especially the division of Eschatology. I remember several times Dr. Crichton saying, "Plagiarism, never! You paid for your schooling. Now go and preach and teach what you have learned!" I did. For over forty years, I have preached and taught what I learned from all my classes, but especially from Dr. Crichton's notes. Over the years I've added multiple notes from my own personal study and notes from many great scholars who authored books on future things. I give credit to the works of:

John Walvoord
Charles Ryrie
Dwight Pentecost
Hal Lindsey
Jack Van Impe
Joel Rosenberg
J. Barton Payne
Michael D. Evans
David Jeremiah
John Hagee
Mark Hitchcock
Grant R. Jeffrey
Sir Robert Anderson
Arnold G. Fruchtenbaum
Tim LaHaye

I'm thankful for the Holy Spirit's insight given these great scholars of the prophetic Word. I believe the Holy Spirit is being poured out on godly men, Messianic Jews, and others to reveal soon-coming prophecy events. I believe God's Holy Spirit is testifying everywhere on earth that God is about to do a great work. It will all start with the Rapture.

Terry Burnside

Table of Contents

ONE

An Overview of Prophecy

At that time Joshua pronounced this solemn oath: "Cursed before the LORD is the one who undertakes to rebuild this city, Jericho: At the cost of his firstborn son he will lay its foundations; at the cost of his youngest he will set up its gates." So the LORD was with Joshua, and his fame spread throughout the land. (Joshua 6:26-27)

In this chapter we will look at an overview of prophecy. We will see why Joshua's words in Joshua 6:26-27 are so important to understand prophecy.

Let me give you the definition of prophecy. Theologically, it is the divine revelation of future events. When you mention the word *revelation* you also have to mention two other words: inspiration and illumination. How does the Word of God get to you and me? How does it get to your soul and my soul? How does it get to your heart and my heart? The Sovereign Lord God in His providence and plan, His counsel, and His will, chose a process. The process is revelation, inspiration, and illumination.

From the mind of God to the mind of the prophet is revelation. Revelation is the communication of truth; the truth of God. From the mind of the prophet to the written page is inspiration. Inspiration is the infallible recording and perpetuation of God's truth. From the written page to your mind and my mind is illumination. Illumination is the elucidation, explanation, and enlightenment of God's truth. In illumination, we are asking the Holy Spirit of God to guide us into all truth. That is my heart's desire for this book. The Holy Spirit is our Teacher.

So, prophecy is the divine revelation of future events. This is the theological definition of prophecy. We know God has revealed Himself in nature (Psalm 19). God has also revealed Himself in His Word. We call this special revelation. It is specific revelation. Isaiah 46:10 says, "I make known the end from the beginning, from ancient times, what is still to come. I say: My purpose will stand, and *I will* do all that I please." God doesn't say, "I make known the beginning to the end." God says, "I make known the end from the beginning." God chose to make known to us eternal truths. His plans, thoughts, and ways are made known to us in His Word. Let's glorify Him. Revelation 4:11 says, "You are worthy, our Lord and God, to receive glory and honor and power, for you created all things, and by your will they were created and have their being." All things were created by God's will. His purpose, counsel, and will stand, and He will do all He pleases. When the Word of God was written, and we know it was written over a period of 1,600 years by forty or so different human authors, it was twenty-seven percent prophetic. When the Bible was penned, twenty-seven percent of what was written down awaited fulfillment. Much of what was written was history, poetry, prose, and narrative. However, almost one-third was still prophecy, and one-third of that prophecy concerns the revelation of Jesus Christ and His Millennial Kingdom. It concerns the Second Coming of Jesus Christ and the setting up of His Kingdom on this earth. He *will* establish His Kingdom on earth.

Now, let's merge this definition with the biblical definition. Prophecy is a lamp shining in a dark place. Prophecy is a light shining in the darkness of this world. The dark place is also the future. God has not told us everything. He has not revealed everything about the future. We know this from Deuteronomy 29:29 that says, "The secret things belong to the LORD our God, but the things revealed belong to us and to our children forever, that we may follow all the words of this law." To the extent that God wants us to know about future things, He has revealed these things in His Word. A clear biblical definition of prophecy found in God's Word is where the Apostle Peter emphatically tells us in 2 Peter 1:19-21:

> We also have the prophetic message as something completely reliable, and you will do well to pay attention to it, as to a light shining in a dark place, until the day dawns and the morning star rises in your hearts. Above all, you must understand that no prophecy of Scripture came about by the prophet's own interpretation of things. For prophecy never had its origin in the human will, but prophets, though human, spoke from God as they were carried along by the Holy Spirit.

God's Word gives us light. Light conquers the darkness of the human soul. The world can be a dark place. The future can be a dark place. God tells us to pay close attention to the prophetic Word. The day will dawn, and Jesus Christ, the Morning Star, will rise in our hearts.

God has spoken. He has spoken His Word so we may understand. Prophecy is indeed divine revelation. Prophecy did not come about by human ingenuity or design. The authors of the Word of God did not say one day, "Well, I think I will write God's Word today!" No, it didn't happen that way. We believe in the verbal inspiration of the Word of God and its consequent, absolute authority. God caused the human authors of Scripture to write just what He wanted written, yet through their own personalities. Paul told Timothy, "All Scripture is God-breathed and is useful for teaching, rebuking, correcting and training in righteousness, so that the servant of God may be thoroughly equipped for every good work" (2 Timothy 3:16-17). As such, God's Word is without error in all matters and is absolutely authoritative. Jesus said in Matthew 5:17-18,

> Do not think that I have come to abolish the law or the Prophets; I have not come to abolish them but to fulfill them. For truly I tell you, until heaven and earth disappear, not the smallest letter, not the least stroke of a pen, will by any means disappear from the Law until everything is accomplished.

It is the *jot* and *tittle*. The *jot* refers to the smallest letter in the Hebrew alphabet, the *yod,* and to the smallest letter in the Greek alphabet, the *iota*. The *tittle* is the smallest, slightest stroke of the pen in the Hebrew letters. Jesus said God's Word is authoritative, not only the words, but also the letters; even the smallest letters making up the words and even the slightest stroke of the pen is from God. In the original manuscripts, written by the forty or so human authors, the message from God is the absolute authority as the authors were carried along by the Holy Spirit of God as they wrote down His Word. God used the authors' personalities, their backgrounds, and their unique styles of writing. When they wrote the Word of God, it was not man's words. It was from God. They spoke by the mouth of the Holy Spirit of God. See Appendix A for "The Bible—Man's Authority."

My practical definition of prophecy is God's history written in advance. Only God, the Eternal One, could reveal truth to us with such precision and accuracy that many prophecies were fulfilled in complete detail, and we know that the remaining prophecies awaiting fulfillment will be fulfilled in His timing. God is the Author of all history. Prophecy is God's history written down for us to know His sovereign plan of the ages. "I make known the end from the beginning, from ancient times, what is still to come. I say, 'My purpose will stand, and I will do all that I please'" (Isaiah 46:10).

To understand future events, we must have a good grasp of prophecy itself. Joshua 6:26-27 is one of many strange prophecies of the Old Testament. Joshua's prophecy concerning Jericho is fulfilled in 1 Kings 16:29-34. Joshua gave this prophecy in 1400 B.C., and it was fulfilled in 874 B.C., exactly 526 years later. It was fulfilled literally. Literalness is important to understand all prophecies. See Appendix B for an Outline on Prophecy and Scriptures.

On the day that Jesus Christ died for our sins on the Cross of Calvary, thirty-three prophecies were fulfilled. You will find the list of the prophecies fulfilled in one day in Appendix C, "Thirty-three Prophecies Fulfilled in One Day." For one prophecy to come to pass on one particular day is amazing in itself, but to have thirty-three prophecies fulfilled in just one day is overwhelming proof that God's Word is His promise. See Appendix C. Also read Luke 24.

We then have a theological, biblical, and practical definition of prophecy. Theologically, prophecy concerns future events. It is God's divine revelation concerning future things. Biblically, prophecy is a lamp; a light that shines in a dark place. The dark place is the future. It also refers to the darkness of this world system of sin. The practical definition of prophecy is God's history written in advance. It is God's description of future things.

We see the relationship between eschatology and prophecy. Eschatology is a branch or division of prophecy. Eschatology is the last word. God is going to have the last word. Eschatology is the study of future, final, and last things. Eschatology concerns itself with events beyond this present age, beyond the Church Age, beyond this present life, and beyond death. We say, "Why does that concern us?" As we will see in this book, it concerns us greatly. The question will be asked, "Where will we spend eternity?" Our answer, and why we answer the way we do, determines our eternal destiny. We will only hear what God has spoken. He has spoken in these days through His Son. The author of Hebrews says, "In the past God spoke to our ancestors through the prophets at many times and in various ways, but in these last days he has spoken to us by his Son, whom he appointed heir of all things, and through whom also he made the universe" (Hebrews 1:1-2). I say that concerns us. What will you do with Jesus? You cannot be neutral. One day your soul will be asking, "What will He do with me?"

There are prophecies in the Old Testament (some strange, see Appendix B) that came to fulfillment. Many prophecies from the Old Testament await fulfillment. God has made many promises to us. I've heard Bible scholars say there are up to ten thousand promises in the Word of God for the believer. I don't know the exact number, but all God's promises are true and yes in Jesus Christ. The Apostle Paul declared boldly to the church at Corinth, "For no matter how many promises God has made, they are 'Yes' in Christ. And so through him the 'Amen' is spoken by us to the glory of God" (2 Corinthians 1:20). The promises of God find there answer in Jesus. Jesus is the reason why not one word of all God's good promises has failed or fallen to the ground. God is going to fulfill His Word. However, so much more awaits God's timing to be accomplished. I conclude this overview of prophecy with these words in 1 Kings 8:56, "Praise be to the LORD, who has given rest to his people Israel just as he promised. Not one word has failed of all the good promises he gave through his servant Moses."

Bibles opened? Highlighters ready? Let's begin.

Note: A great resource on the subject matter of this chapter is the work by J. Barton Payne, *The Encyclopedia of Biblical Prophecy*.

TWO

The Great Trumpeting Translation

> Do not let your hearts be troubled. You believe in God;
> believe also in me. My Father's house has many rooms; if
> that were not so, would I have told you that I am going
> there to prepare a place for you? And if I go and prepare
> a place for you, I will come back and take you to be with
> me that you also may be where I am. You know the way
> to the place where I am going. (John 14:1-4)

These verses are familiar to us and bring a great source of comfort, as they did for Jesus' disciples. Let's start now looking at The Great Trumpeting Translation. This begins our study of optimistic prophecy. I call it optimistic prophecy because God is sovereign, and He will fulfill His Word. I'm optimistic about the next event on God's prophetic calendar: the next event is the Rapture. I'm optimistic because Jesus is returning, perhaps today. I love the word Rapture! My favorite subject in the Word of God is the Rapture. I love the truth that Jesus said He is coming again and I believe that He will.

God's promises are true and find embodiment in Jesus Christ and He is God's answer: not one word of all His good promises have failed or fallen to the ground (1 Kings 8:56). Look again in John 14. What did Jesus say in verse three? "And if I go and prepare a place for you, I will come back and take you to be with me that you also may be where I am." When did Jesus make that statement? He made it on the eve of His crucifixion in the Upper Room with His disciples. Their hearts were troubled, and He said don't let your hearts be troubled. You believe in Jehovah God, believe in Me. Because in My Father's House there are many rooms, many mansions, many dwelling places. I go there to prepare the way for you, and a place for you, and I am going to come back (John 14:1-3). Do you believe that? This is optimistic prophecy. Do you know why I am an optimist? I have read the final words of the Bible in Revelation, chapter 22. Jesus said He would come quickly: He said He would be coming soon. Even so, come quickly and soon, Lord Jesus! The grace of our Lord Jesus Christ will be with all of us. Amen and Amen!

Jesus said He will come back and take us to where He is: that's optimism, and I believe that. The coming of Jesus Christ has been the expectation of the Church since her beginning. It has been the excitement of the Church; it has been the enthusiasm of the Church that Jesus Christ is coming back again. The scriptures that deal specifically with that are John 14, 1 Thessalonians 4, and 1 Corinthians 15. My favorite passage in God's Word is 1 Thessalonians 4. For centuries creeds, such as the Apostles' Creed, have included the tenet (based on passages from God's Word such as 1 Thessalonians 4) that Jesus Christ, who now sits at the right hand of God the Father Almighty, will come back from Heaven.

Let's look at The Great Trumpeting Translation. On God's prophetic clock, the Rapture is imminent: it can take place at any time. Would you mind if the Rapture took place today? *It could happen today!* Jesus Christ will come back again. The world scenario today is troubling. What should our response be to the outcries of our world? The invitation from God is to come to Jesus Christ for repentance, forgiveness, and fullness of salvation (Revelation 22:17). Be ready for life and death: be ready to serve God by serving others (John 21:2-25). Jesus is coming (Hebrews 10:37). Are you ready? Are you prepared? The message of the Rapture is to the saved and the lost; it should be the defining message of the Church of Jesus Christ today.

The message of the Rapture should be forefront as we share the good news of the gospel of Jesus Christ's death, burial, resurrection, and ascension into Heaven. Jesus has made this great promise, "And if I go and prepare a place for you, I will come back and take you to be with me that you also may be where I am" (John 14:3). His Return at the Rapture is called translation. Translation means to transfer from one place to another. It is an act of removal, and a change will be involved. There are four great translations in the Word of God. Three are physical and one is spiritual. Two are found in the Old Testament, having to do with what happened to Enoch and Elijah. These men are called types of the Rapture. A type is a divinely purposed illustration which prefigures and corresponds to its present reality. A type is a living prediction, pattern, or model of one who is to come, or what is to come. In the Old Testament God gave many, many types. Most point to Jesus Christ, but what happened to these two men, Enoch and Elijah, are types of the Rapture. They point to this event that I call The Great Trumpeting Translation. Enoch and Elijah are patterns of what it will be like on that day when Jesus Christ returns.

First, let's look at Enoch. Much is said about Enoch. Enoch was the very first prophet. He was the first person to prophesy about the Second Coming of Jesus Christ. In the book of Jude (Jude was the half-brother of our Lord Jesus Christ), Jude said Enoch prophesied that the Lord is coming with thousands upon thousands of His holy ones, His angels, to judge the ungodly (Jude 14). Enoch descended from Adam and through Seth (God gave Adam and Eve another son after Cain murdered his brother Abel). He was the seventh generation from Adam. Enoch's father was Jared, and he had a son named Methuselah. Methuselah lived 969 years (Adam only lived 930 years), but Enoch did not live as long as Adam or his father Jared. Enoch only lived 365 years. The Word of God teaches us that he walked with God, and one day he was no more because God took him. God translated him (Genesis 5:18-24). Look at Hebrews 11, the great faith chapter, verse 5. It reads, "By faith Enoch was taken from this life, so that he did not experience death: 'He could not be found, because God had taken him away.' For before he was taken, he was commended as one who pleased God."

Let's understand the parallel. Since Enoch is a type, the antitype is the Rapture, The Great Trumpeting Translation. There will be a period of time at the Rapture when a whole generation of believers world-wide will not experience death. All living believers, if the Rapture happened right now, would not experience death. Also, we will not experience the horrible persecution of the Tribulation. We may have to walk through the valley of the shadow of death (Psalm 23), but how wonderful it would be to be like Enoch and not experience death.

Enoch could not be found because God had taken him away. What did Jesus say? "I will come back to receive you to Myself and take you back where I am." That's what happened to Enoch because, before he was taken, he was commended as one who pleased God. That's why we are to live for Jesus Christ. He could come back at any time. Our lives should be like Enoch's, commended as people who please God. So, Enoch is a type of the Rapture. His was the first physical translation in the Word of God.

The second physical translation is Elijah in 2 Kings, chapter 2. God revealed to Elijah that he would be taken up into Heaven in a whirlwind. I guess the Rapture will be like that. When the Christian dead rise, tons of dust will be disturbed and unsettled. A whirlwind, a fiery chariot, and horses of fire; *oh, my!*

Elijah and Elisha went from Gilgal to Bethel to Jericho to the Jordon River. Elijah took his cloak and struck the Jordan River, and the waters divided and stood up to the right and to the left. They both crossed over on dry ground (God had His people cross over on dry ground several times in Scripture). Elijah and Enoch got to the other side and continued normal activities of the day, walking and talking. All of a sudden, the fiery chariot and horses of fire appeared separating Elijah from Elisha. Elisha saw Elijah no more. God had taken Elijah. "Elisha saw this and cried out, 'My father! My father! The chariots and horsemen of Israel!' And Elisha saw him no more. Then he took hold of his garment and tore it in two" (2 Kings 2:12).

God had translated Elijah. This physical translation is also a type of the Church being raptured. Elijah did not experience death. Again, there will be a period of time at the Rapture when a whole generation of believers world-wide will not experience death. All living

24

believers, if the Rapture happened right now, would not experience death. Elijah's translation is a type of the Rapture.

The third translation that is found in the Word of God is in Colossians 1:12-14. It is a spiritual translation called regeneration. It reads,

> And giving joyful thanks to the Father, who has quali-
> fied you to share in the inheritance of his holy people
> in the kingdom of light. For he has rescued us from the
> dominion of darkness and brought us into the kingdom
> of the Son he loves, in whom we have redemption, the
> forgiveness of sins.

"Brought us" is rendered "translated us" in the King James Version. It is in Jesus Christ that we have redemption and forgiveness of sin. When we receive Jesus Christ as our Lord and Savior, we are immediately transferred from the kingdom of darkness to the kingdom of Jesus Christ. We are transferred from one place to another, from death to life because change has taken place that the Bible calls repentance. Repentance is a change of mind, heart, and will. God alone can accomplish the spiritual translation of salvation found only in His Son, Jesus Christ. Praise the Father! Praise the Son! Praise the Holy Spirit! This happens every time someone accepts Jesus Christ as Lord and Savior. The Apostle Paul gave his personal testimony in front of King Herod Agrippa in Acts 26:15-18,

> Then I asked, "Who are you, Lord?" "I am Jesus, whom
> you are persecuting," the Lord replied. "Now get up and
> stand on your feet. I have appeared to you to appoint you
> as a servant and as a witness of what you have seen and
> will see of me. I will rescue you from your own people
> and from the Gentiles. I am sending you to them to open
> their eyes and turn them from darkness to light, and from
> the power of Satan to God, so that they may receive for-
> giveness of sins and a place among those who are sancti-
> fied by faith in me."

This spiritual translation is the first translation of the saint in Jesus Christ, the first translation of Church Age believers. We are turned from the kingdom of darkness to the kingdom of light. God does that through the gospel message. It works every time someone receives Jesus. We are in the Kingdom of God, God's spiritual, eternal Kingdom.

The fourth translation is another physical translation. It is called the Rapture. Today, the Church Age saints participate in the spiritual translation of regeneration (being born again). In the future, at the coming and presence of Jesus Christ, we will experience the physical translation, the Rapture.

First, the nature of the Rapture is, in essence, God completing His work of redemption in the life of the believer, the Church Age saint. Sin does three things to man. It brings guilt, pollution, and mortality. In our consciences, we are guilty. In our nature, we are polluted. We are depraved. I believe in total depravity. Man cannot save himself. Man is totally depraved: body, soul, and spirit. Man cannot do anything to save himself. No work, no matter how good, can save man. Ultimately, we die. This is mortality. Romans 6:23 says, "For the wages of sin is death, but the gift of God is eternal life in Christ Jesus our Lord." God's salvation includes deliverance from the penalty, power, and presence of sin. These are three great doctrines in God's Word concerning our salvation: justification, sanctification, and glorification. I can say that I have been saved, I am being saved, and I shall be saved. Justification means "pronounced righteous." We are saved by the washing of regeneration and renewing by the Holy Spirit of God (Titus 3:5). It is not by our own righteousness or what we have done. Through justification, God saves us from the pollution, penalty, and guilt of sin. Praise God for justification!

Sanctification is the process of dying to self each day, taking up your cross and following Christ. Sin's power needs to be broken each day. Sanctification breaks the power of sin in our life. You cannot count on yesterday's victories for today's triumphs. I can be saved from the power of sin as I yield my life to the Holy Spirit of God. When I am controlled by the Holy Spirit, then I do not grieve or quench the Holy Spirit's work in my life. Sanctification is God setting us apart to Himself. It is a life of holiness. It is keeping short accounts with God. It is practicing daily. First John 1:9 states: "If we confess our sins, he

26

is faithful and just and will forgive us our sins and purify us from all unrighteousness."

Glorification is being saved from the very presence of sin. There will be no more sin when we get to Heaven. Glorification is the completion of God's redemptive work in the life of the believer. God has begun a good work in us, and He will complete it. Paul told the church at Philippi, "Being confident of this, that he who began a good work in you will carry it on to completion until the day of Christ Jesus" (Philippians 1:6). We will be saved for glorification on the day of our Lord Jesus Christ's appearing at the Rapture, or, if we die before He comes. Scriptures teach us that a Christian who is absent from the body is present with the Lord Jesus Christ (2 Corinthians 5:8). We will be saved to the uttermost! That's what the Rapture will do for the Body of Jesus Christ.

Second, what is the Rapture? The definition of the Rapture is that event in which the Church, both dead and living saints, will be translated from earth to meet the Lord Jesus Christ in the air, and then be taken back with Him to Heaven. You cannot find the word Rapture in the Word of God. You also cannot find the word *Trinity* in the Bible, nor can you find the words *Bible*, *Christianity*, or *Millennium*. While the words cannot be found, the doctrine is taught in the Word of God and presented in many passages that we will look at together. The Church of Jesus Christ has used these words over many centuries.

The word *Rapture* has been used by the Church to refer to being caught up. Paul speaks of this in 1 Thessalonians 4:17, "After that, we who are still alive and are left will be caught up together with them in the clouds to meet the Lord in the air. And so we will be with the Lord forever." "Caught up" comes from the Latin word *rapio* which translates "to be snatched away." The verb conveys the idea of force suddenly exercised. It is a forceful seizure, to snatch or catch away. The Greek word used is *harpazo*. God is going to snatch you and me quickly to meet Jesus in the air. We will be carried off, caught up, snatched, and grasped hastily by the appearing of Jesus Christ. The translation from *harpazo* to the word Rapture involved two steps: first, *harpazo* from the Greek became the Latin word *rapio*. Second, *rapio* became our English word for Rapture.

Third, what is the time of Rapture? The Rapture is imminent. It is at hand. Jesus says He is coming quickly three times in Revelation, chapter 22. The Greek word is *tachu*. It means all these words: quickly, suddenly, imminently, speedily, shortly, hastily, readily, soon, and without delay.

Now, let's look at proofs of the Pre-tribulation Rapture position:

1. Consider Revelation 3:10

The promise of promises is presented. Exemption from the Day of the Lord's wrath is promised. The special hour of world-wide trial will occur on the earth for seven years. We are kept out of this time period according to Revelation 3:10, "Since you have kept my command to endure patiently, I will also keep you from the hour of trial that is going to come on the whole world to test the inhabitants of the earth." It does not say we are kept *through*, which is *preservation*. There is an *evacuation*. The Church will be gone when the terrible hour of Tribulation's judgment comes on the world to try the earth dwellers. This is an internal proof in the Book of Revelation for the Rapture occurring before the Tribulation hour begins.

2. Consider the Church in the Book of Revelation

Another internal proof in the Book of Revelation is the word Church itself. The Greek word is *ekklesia*, the Church of Jesus Christ, a calling out, an assembly. We are the called out, assembled ones. We are the Christian community on earth. Saints on earth and in Heaven are represented in the Church:
- Ephesians 3:14-15 and Romans 14:7-9.
- The Church of Jesus Christ is mentioned twenty times in the Book of Revelation, nineteen times in chapters 1-3 and one time in chapter 22, verse 16.
- Where is the Church of Jesus Christ in chapters 4-5? The Rapture has already taken place, and we are with Jesus Christ in Heaven in chapters 4 and 5!

- Where is the Church of Jesus Christ in chapters 6-18? The Church of Jesus Christ is not on the earth. We are in Heaven! The Church cannot be found in the Book of Revelation during any part of the Tribulation.

3. Consider Revelation 4

This is another internal proof of the Pre-tribulation Rapture in the Book of Revelation, chapter 4, concerning the twenty-four elders.

The Levitical Priesthood was divided into twenty-four groups for priestly ministry. According to 1 Chronicles, chapters 15 and 16, David rearranged the Levitical priesthood into twenty-four courses (groups). Today, Christians are the royal priesthood (1 Peter 2:9) and are represented by the twenty-four elders. The scene in Heaven, chapters 4 and 5, pictures what happens immediately after the Rapture.

4. Consider "the time of Jacob's trouble"

Jacob is Israel, as shown in Jeremiah 30:7, "How awful that day will be! No other will be like it. It will be a time of trouble for Jacob, but he will be saved out of it." See also Romans 11:26.

5. Consider "Daniel's Seventieth Week"

In Daniel 9:24-27, Israel experiences the trials of the future. The Tribulation is "Daniel's seventieth week." The first sixty-nine weeks of the Prophecy of the Seventy Weeks involved Israel (Daniel 9). The seventieth week will also involve Israel. Why would the final week revert to the Church of Jesus Christ?

6. Consider the Hinderer ... the Holy Spirit

As shown in 2 Thessalonians 2:1-8, the Day of the Lord cannot come until a departure from the faith occurs and the lawless one, the super deceiver, is revealed. The Antichrist will not be manifested until the One who restrains his appearing is removed—the Holy Spirit.

7. Consider God's promises to exempt us from wrath

In 1 Thessalonians 1:10; 5:9; Romans 5:9, the Greek word is *orge*, meaning, punishment, vengeance, and indignation. Christian suffering is different, involving trials, testings, chastisement, and discipline.

See 1 Peter 4:1; 5:10. The Greek word is *pascho,* meaning to experience pain, to vex.

8. Consider God's deliverance of His people in the past

- **Noah and the flood**
  Genesis 6; Hebrews 11:7; 1 Peter 3:20
- **Lot and Lot's daughters**
  2 Peter 2:4-8; Genesis 19
- **Daniel's three friends in the fiery furnace**
  Daniel 3; Hebrews 11:33-34
- **Daniel in the lions' den**
  Daniel 6; Hebrews 11:33-34

What I see in all these events is that they reveal that the righteous did not have to suffer with the unrighteous.

9. Consider Dr. Randall Johnson's position (on staff at Central Church in Collierville, Tennessee)

The most compelling argument (in defense of the Pre-tribulation Rapture position) to me is that, if it is Post-tribulation, that means every believer entering the kingdom is glorified, meaning they are no longer capable of reproducing children. Unless unbelievers are allowed to enter the kingdom (they are not), there is, therefore, no one to repopulate the earth with children who stand in need of individual conversion, but who may choose instead to reject Christ and later be allied by Satan to attack Jerusalem (Revelation 20).

10. Consider Dr. Bill Bellican's position (on staff at Central Church in Collierville, Tennessee)

> What comfort would there be for a new Christian if you tell them after they are saved that they have to go through seven years of Tribulation (outside of dying before the Tribulation begins)? There is not much comfort to be found in Post-tribulation teaching. Yes, believers during this age who live godly in Christ Jesus will suffer persecution, but this is vastly different from The Great Tribulation spoken of by prophets and Christ Jesus Himself.

11. Consider the biblical Jewish marriage customs and analogy with John 14

See Appendix D for a complete explanation of *Behold the Bridegroom Comes,* by Dr. Renald Showers.

See Appendix E for a short play written by me and adapted from *Behold the Bridegroom Comes,* by Dr. Renald Showers. Feel free to perform it in any setting!

The above proofs are very definitive for the Pre-tribulation Rapture position. But, let me give the other positions. The Mid-tribulation Rapture position teaches that the Rapture will occur three and one-half years into the Tribulation, at the beginning of the three and one-half year Great Tribulation. The Post-tribulation Rapture position teaches that the Rapture will not occur until the end of the seven year Tribulation, just prior to the beginning of the Millennial Kingdom. Enthusiastically, I hold to the Pre-tribulation Rapture position. It is my approach to prophecy, especially the Book of Revelation. Pre-tribulation and Pre-millennial is the way to view eschatology through the lens of the literal interpretation of God's Word, especially prophecy yet to be fulfilled.

Fourth, what are the events of the Rapture? God has divinely revealed them to us in 1 Thessalonians 4:13-18:

> Brothers and sisters, we do not want you to be uninformed about those who sleep in death, so that you do not grieve like the rest of mankind, who have no hope. For we believe that Jesus died and rose again, and so we believe that God will bring with Jesus those who have fallen asleep in him. According to the Lord's word, we tell you that we who are still alive, who are left until the coming of the Lord, will certainly not precede those who have fallen asleep. For the Lord himself will come down from heaven, with a loud command, with the voice of the archangel, and the trumpet call of God, and the dead in Christ will rise first. After that, we who are still alive and are left will be caught up together with them in the clouds to meet the Lord in the air. And so we will be with the Lord forever. Therefore encourage one another with these words.

The return of Jesus Christ is presented for us. This passage speaks of the coming of the Lord. At His coming, He will come down from Heaven, and the resurrection of the Christian dead takes place. God will bring back with Jesus all those who have died in Christ from the day of Pentecost (the coming of the Holy Spirit and the birth of the Church) to the day of the Rapture. Jesus brings their spirits with Him. Their bodies rise first and reunite with their spirits. If we are still alive at that moment, then we will be raptured. This is the Rapture of the living saints. At that moment, a whole generation of believers will not die. We are caught up together, meaning the reunion of dead and living saints. Hallelujah! Now, the hallelujah gets louder, for we have the realization of the Lord's presence. It is the Lord Jesus Christ who promised He would come back to receive us to Himself. There is unity of the Body of Christ, completely together to share the joy of our Lord Jesus Christ forever. First Corinthians 15:50-53 says,

> I declare to you, brothers and sisters, that flesh and blood cannot inherit the kingdom of God, nor does the perishable inherit the imperishable. Listen, I tell you a mystery: We will not all sleep, but we will all be changed—in a flash, in the twinkling of an eye, at the last trumpet. For the trumpet will sound, the dead will be raised imperishable, and we will be changed. For the perishable must clothe itself with the imperishable, and the mortal with immortality.

Paul told the church in Corinth that flesh and blood cannot inherit the kingdom of God. I cannot go to Heaven in my mortal body as I look today in my physical, perishable, and corruptible body. No one can. Paul called the Rapture a mystery. Mystery in Scripture is a truth unknown and unknowable apart from God's divine revelation. The mystery revealed is that believers will not die when the Rapture takes place. Just by reading Genesis 5 about Enoch and 2 Kings 2 about Elijah, we would not have known that an entire generation of Christians would not die when the Rapture happens. God revealed His plan further, and now we know that we must be changed and we will be changed at the Rapture. We will be changed in a flash—in a moment. The Greek word for flash is the negative alpha, "a" plus the word "tempo" which means to cut. *Atempo* means impossible to cut or slice any thinner.

Atempo is where we get our word "atom." Upon discovering the atom, scientists named it atom from the Greek *atempo*. Scientists thought the atom was so small it was impossible to cut any further. The atom, however, has been cut up into parts. The scientists were wrong. God's Word is never wrong. The Rapture will happen in a period of time so fast that it is impossible to slice it any thinner. The Rapture will happen just like that. Jesus Christ will come back, and we will be gone!

The second expression conveyed to us in *atempo* tells us the speed with which the Rapture will take place. It is in the twinkling of an eye. Scientists say you can blink your eye in about one-tenth of a second. The word in the Greek, though, refers to the buzz of a gnat, the quivering of a harp string, and the twinkling of a star. This is how swift it is going to take place. At that moment there will be no time to accept Jesus Christ as your Lord and Savior. If you have not received God's gift of salvation before, 'you will be left out and left to go into the Great Tribulation that shall come upon all the earth for seven years.

Please consider the following:

Gospel Presentation:

I have found that most people are interested in spiritual things. Do you know for certain that you are going to Heaven? Are you sure? Please consider carefully what is presented now from God's Word. God is speaking to your heart right now. Have you trusted Jesus Christ alone for your salvation? Hear from God now.

Heaven … there is only one way to get there.

What does the Bible say about Heaven?
John 14:6: "Jesus answered, 'I am the way and the truth and the life. No one comes to the Father except through me.'"

We have sinned.

Our sin stops us from going to Heaven.
Romans 3:23: "For all have sinned and fall short of the glory of God."

God loves us.

God wants us to be with Him in Heaven.
John 3:16: "For God so loved the world that he gave his one and only Son, that whoever believes in him shall not perish but have eternal life."

Christ died for us.

His death provides the way for us to go to Heaven.
1 Corinthians 15:3-5: "For what I received I passed on to you as of first importance: that Christ died for our sins according to the Scriptures, that he was buried, that he was raised on the third day according to the Scriptures, and that he appeared to Cephas, and then to the Twelve."

Salvation is a free gift.

God gives this free gift so we may be with Him in Heaven.
Ephesians 2:8-9: "For it is by grace you have been saved, through faith—and this is not from yourselves, it is the gift of God—not by works, so that no one can boast."

We must receive the gift.

God's gift must be received to go to Heaven.
John 1:12: "Yet to all who did receive him, to those who believed in his name, he gave the right to become children of God."

Does this make sense to you?

Would you like to receive the gift of eternal life, God's free gift of salvation, and to know you will be going to Heaven? If you do, you will be receiving eternal life!

You may pray this prayer:

Dear God,

I know I am a sinner. I believe your Son Jesus Christ died on the cross for my sins. I now repent and turn from my sins and open my heart to ask Jesus Christ to come in and save me from my sins. Give me eternal life. I thank you Lord Jesus for being in my heart and giving me eternal life in Heaven with you.

I pray in Jesus Christ's Name. Amen.

If you prayed that prayer, you have been born again by God's Holy Spirit. Praise God!

Assurance:

John 6:47: "Very truly I tell you, the one who believes has eternal life."

1 John 5:11-13: "And this is the testimony: God has given us eternal life, and this life is in his Son. Whoever has the Son has life; whoever does not have the Son of God does not have life. I write

these things to you who believe in the name of the Son of God so that you may know that you have eternal life."

I pray at this very moment you know beyond a shadow of a doubt that you have made the greatest decision there is to make in life: trusting Jesus Christ alone for your salvation and eternal life.

Read Appendix F—"Salvation and the Cross—God's Remedy and Man's Hope."

I pray now you are ready for the Rapture. First Thessalonians 4 shares the residence of believers with the Lord, and it will be forever. I'm a literalist. Forever means forever. Forever we will be with the Lord. No wonder this is such a great source of comfort as we encourage each other with these words. After the Rapture, wherever Christ is and whatever Christ is doing, that is where we will be and what we will be doing! The Church of Jesus Christ, His Bride, will be eternally married to Him (Revelation 19:1-8) and the wedding reception (wedding feast or supper in Revelation 19:9) will be held on the earth. We will co-reign with our Lord and Savior during His Kingdom reign over the earth for 1,000 years. We will spend eternity with Him. O blissful thought! O sweet reality! Hallelujah!

Paul says in 2 Corinthians 6:2, "For he says, 'In the time of my favor I heard you, and in the day of salvation I helped you.' I tell you, now is the time of God's favor, now is the day of salvation." Today is the day of salvation. The Church of Jesus Christ worldwide has the greatest message ever told to share with all people everywhere. It is the good news of what Jesus Christ has done for us. The Church of Jesus Christ today also needs to tell the rest of the story loudly and clearly. We reach, connect, equip, and go. The process is repeated over and over again. People need the Lord. The world scenario today is troubling. The Rapture of the Church is imminent. We should be so missionary-minded that the world may hear what God has to say about receiving eternal life. What should our response be to the outcries of our world? The world is crying for help. We can give them the Living Bread of Life, Jesus Christ. We need to share that He is coming. Are you ready? Are you prepared?

This message is to the saved and the lost. If you are saved, Jesus is coming. If you have yet to come to Christ, He is still coming. It could be today! There is so much teaching in Scripture on the

Second Coming of Christ, both Rapture and Revelation. Personally, I've always believed I would be part of the Rapture generation. Church of Jesus Christ, share loudly and clearly today that Jesus Christ could come at any moment. That is enough motivation to reach the world for Christ. Teach and preach the Rapture. God will be honored and glorified. The Apostles' Creed has stated for centuries "whence He shall come to judge the living and the dead." Make Jesus Christ known, past, present, and future.

From what we have already read, we have seen that the Rapture is the next event on God's prophetic program. It is a physical translation. We have seen that the Church Age saints participate in the spiritual translation of regeneration and, in the future, the translation at the coming and presence of Jesus Christ. The view presented in this book is *Pre-tribulational. I am conservative in my approach to prophecy. Other approaches are not so literal.* I hold to the futurist approach that teaches that Chapters 4-22 in the Book of Revelation deal with predictive prophecy instead of fulfilled prophecy. These chapters in the Book of Revelation deal with prophetic events yet to occur.

The futurist teaches that the principles found in prophecy, especially the Book of Revelation, are applicable to the Church today. This is true of all Scripture. Paul told Timothy in 2 Timothy 3:16-17, "All Scripture is God-breathed and is useful for teaching, rebuking, correcting and training in righteousness, so that the servant of God may be thoroughly equipped for every good work."

The Tribulation Period is covered extensively in Revelation. I believe in the literal view. I teach that the seven great and true future events are just that, future events that have not yet been fulfilled. It is the futurist position. Other approaches are the symbolic, preterist, and historical. The historical view teaches that the major events in Revelation parallel with actual history at different times and generations, but the book still contains good principles to be taught today. The preterist view teaches that almost everything in prophecy, especially the Book of Revelation, has already occurred during the first two or three centuries after Christ. The symbolic view teaches that Revelation is allegory only. Revelation, according to the allegorist, is full of symbols portraying the conflict between

God and Satan. They also teach there is no specific, literal event in Revelation. I agree with the futurist position. I am Pre-tribulational and Pre-millennial. Now, let's take a quick look at the teaching of the three main views concerning the Millennium.

Amillennialists teach that the Millennium is spiritual and the Church today is *Spiritual Israel*. The letter "**a**" in front of the word Amillennial negates the literalness of the one thousand years. Amillennialists do not believe in a literal Millennial Kingdom. There is no literal one thousand-year Kingdom of God on earth ruled by Jesus Christ. They believe the promise of the Kingdom is fulfilled in the Church during the present Church Age. Followers of this view hold that Christ currently reigns in the hearts of Christians and that there is no need for a physical reign. The future reign with Christ described in Revelation 20 is considered to be ruling with Christ in Heaven and not on earth. Because there are promises to Israel that are to take place in the Millennial Kingdom, this view holds that the promises to Israel have been transferred to the Church. This is why they teach the Church today is *Spiritual Israel*.

Also, the Amillennialist teaches that the covenants in the Old Testament, the Abrahamic, Palestinian, Davidic, and New Covenants are being fulfilled spiritually in the Church today. Israel rejected Jesus Christ as her Messiah, and that is a final rejection according to this teaching. God is done with Israel as they have rejected their Messiah. This teaching is Covenant or Reformed theology. It teaches that God has abandoned the promises made to the Jews and has replaced the Jews with Christians as His chosen people on the earth. Covenant theologians argue that they have not denied that God abandoned His promises to Israel. Rather, they see the fulfillment of the promises to Israel in the person and the work of the Messiah, Jesus Christ. They teach the covenant blessings have been passed to the Church of Jesus Christ. For the Reformed theologian, the Church is *Spiritual Israel*. Even though they would deny that this is not a separate replacement entity, it still seems that they believe God is finished with Israel now and, in the future, only working through the Church.

I hold to Dispensational Theology. Dispensational Theology teaches that God has worked in different dispensations or ages. Its name reflects a view that biblical history is best understood as a series of dispensations, or separated time periods, in the Bible. Each dispensation is said to represent a different way in which God deals with man. Dispensationalism is an evangelical, futurist approach in interpreting God's Word. God related to His creation in different periods of history. God extended His favor toward man, but as in all ages, man turned from His grace and utterly fell short of the glory of God (Romans 3:23). Our present time is the Age of Grace, the Age of the Church of Jesus Christ, and the Age of the Holy Spirit.

The Post-millennial view holds that Christ will return at the end of the Millennial Kingdom. The gospel will be preached to the whole world. The world will be Christianized. To the Post-millennialist, after this happens, Jesus will have to return. So, through the spread of the gospel, the world will continue to get better and better until the Church *conquers the world* so to speak. At the culmination of all things, Jesus will return to judge the world, sending the wicked to Hell and the righteous to their reward. During this time, sin will not cease, but it will be minimized because of the influence of the Church. Christ will not physically reign, but rather, He will spiritually reign through the Church, because of its vast influence over all facets of life. Post-millennialists teach that Christ would not need to reign if the Church ruled by following His principles. According to their teaching, the world will witness unprecedented peace as Isaiah 65:20 is realized, "Never again will there be in it an infant who lives but a few days, or an old man who does not live out his years; the one who dies at a hundred will be thought a mere child; the one who fails to reach a hundred will be considered accursed." The thousand year period does not have to be a literal thousand years. It may be figurative to simply mean a long period of time. Like the Amillennial view, this view sees the promises to Israel as being fulfilled spiritually with the Church. God is finished with Israel because of their rejection. This view enjoyed heightened popularity during the Industrial Revolution in America and England when people saw the world getting better and better and the gospel reaching further and further into the world. In the twentieth century, many left this view because two World Wars ruined their optimism for a better world.

The Pre-millennial view holds that Christ will return to begin a period of time known as the Millennial Kingdom as described in Revelation 20. While other views are still considered orthodox and biblically based, this view is regarded as the most literal interpretation. Opponents argue that apocalyptic literature cannot and should not be taken literally. I disagree. The Pre-millennial view holds to a literal reign of Christ on David's throne. Resurrected and glorified saints will reign with Christ during this time. Many consider this time to be a literal thousand years, although one may hold to this view without believing in a literal Millennium, but rather just an extended period of time. I do not hold to its being an extended period of time. It is a literal, one thousand-year period. During this time Satan is bound and holds no sway over humanity on the earth. At the end of the one thousand years, he will be released, and then conquered once and for all as he is thrown into the lake of fire. When Satan is bound for one thousand years, the world will witness unprecedented peace as Isaiah 65:20 is realized. "Never again will there be in it an infant who lives but a few days, or an old man who does not live out his years; the one who dies at a hundred will be thought a mere child; the one who fails to reach a hundred will be considered accursed." During this time, the promises to Israel will finally and completely be fulfilled. This is the only Millennial view that is in line with Dispensationalism as it is the only view that still sees God's continued work with the nation of Israel to bring them to the time of trouble for Israel. Jeremiah 30:7 says, "How awful that day will be! No other will be like it. It will be a time of trouble for Jacob, but he will be saved out of it." It seems in prophecy God is not through with Israel.

The view presented in this book is Pre-tribulational and Pre-millennial. A worthy note to make is that all writings by the early Church apostles, leaders, and fathers until the middle of the Third Century held to the Pre-millennial view of the Second Coming. The future translation at the Rapture will involve our bodies. They are going to have to be changed. The dead in Christ rising first will receive their new bodies, and those of us still alive in our bodies must be changed as well. There is the reunion of living and dead saints. We are caught up in the clouds to meet the Lord in the air. It is the Lord Himself, our Savior, coming back for us. John said in 1 John 3:2, "Dear friends, now we are children of God, and what we will be has not yet been made known. But we know that when he appears, we shall be like him, for we shall see him as he is." I cannot completely describe to you what our new bodies will be like. It is going to be a powerful body, a spiritual body, a glorious body, an imperishable body, and a body of honor, and it will never, never die (1 Corinthians 15). I cannot tell you in detail exactly what it will be like, for that has not been revealed to us. What we do have is the realization of the Lord's presence. We shall always be with the Lord (1 Thessalonians 4:17).

Now, what is our responsibility as believers in the light of the Rapture? First, there is a comforting hope, "Therefore encourage each other with these words" (1 Thessalonians 4:18). Second, there is a purifying hope. John says in 1 John 2:28-3:3,

> And now, dear children, continue in him, so that when he appears we may be confident and unashamed before him at his coming. If you know that he is righteous, you know that everyone who does what is right has been born of him. See what great love the Father has lavished on us, that we should be called children of God! And that is what we are! The reason the world does not know us is that it did not know him. Dear friends, now we are children of God, and what we will be has not yet been made known. But we know that when Christ appears, we shall be like him, for we shall see him as he is. All who have this hope in him purify themselves, just as he is pure.

Third, there is an activating hope spoken by Jesus in Luke 19:13, "So he called ten of his servants and gave them ten minas. 'Put this money to work,' he said, 'until I come back.'"

Let's now look at how the word "rapture" is used in Scripture. We have seen that *harpazo* means to snatch or catch away, a forceful seizure. It is the idea of force suddenly exercised. It means to pluck, pull, or take by force. The word *harpazo* is used in the account of Philip and the Ethiopian eunuch in Acts 8. An angel of the Lord told Philip, the evangelist, to go south on the road from Jerusalem leading to Gaza. On the way, he met an Ethiopian eunuch. If not a full-fledge proselyte (of righteousness) to Judaism through coming fully under Moses' law by circumcision, he was definitely a God-fearer. The eunuch was reading from Isaiah. Philip was invited to get into the chariot. The conversation centered on the Scriptures in Isaiah 53:7-8. Philip began with that Scripture and told the eunuch about Jesus Christ. Upon the Ethiopian eunuch's belief, Philip baptized him. After the baptism, Luke records this in Acts 8:39: "When they came up out of the water, the Spirit of the Lord suddenly took Philip away, and the eunuch did not see him again, but went on his way rejoicing." *Harpazo* is used in the Greek because the Spirit of the Lord suddenly took Philip away. So, it is used in regard to the Spirit of the Lord in catching Philip away.

The word *harpazo* was also used in Paul's life. Paul had a vision. He writes,

> I must go on boasting. Although there is nothing to be gained, I will go on to visions and revelations from the Lord. I know a man in Christ who fourteen years ago was caught up to the third heaven. Whether it was in the body or out of the body I do not know—God knows. And I know that this man—whether in the body or apart from the body I do not know, but God knows—was caught up to paradise and heard inexpressible things, things that no one is permitted to tell. (2 Corinthians 12:1-4)

The word *harpazo* is used when Paul was caught up into Paradise, to the third Heaven.

Harpazo is also used concerning the male child being caught up to God's throne in Revelation 12:5. Revelation 12:5 says, "She gave birth to a son, a male child, 'who will rule all the nations with an iron scepter.' And her child was snatched up to God and to his throne." Israel gave birth to Jesus Christ, the seed of the woman (Genesis 3:15). Jesus ascended into Heaven forty days after His death, burial, and resurrection.

As we have seen, *harpazo* is used for the dead and living saints raptured to Heaven (1 Thessalonians 4:16-17). Acts 1:9-12 says,

> After he said this, he was taken up before their very eyes, and a cloud hid him from their sight. They were looking intently up into the sky as he was going, when suddenly two men dressed in white stood beside them. "Men of Galilee," they said, "why do you stand here looking into the sky? This same Jesus, who has been taken from you into heaven, will come back in the same way you have seen him go into heaven."

The Return of Christ is man's great expectation. Christ's return has been the expectation of believers since the birth of the Church on the Day of Pentecost. Paul would write Titus, "while we wait for the blessed hope—the appearing of the glory of our great God and Savior, Jesus Christ" (Titus 2:13). Man's great expectation is wrapped with the hope of salvation, everlasting life, and the return of Jesus Christ to receive us to Himself. Christ has gone to prepare a place for us in His Father's House. He said He would come again to receive us to Himself, and wherever He is, we will be also (John 14).

Isn't that exciting! Our hope of the glorious appearing of our great God and Savior Jesus Christ should stir our souls. It is a comforting, purifying, and activating hope. Paul told the church of Thessalonica that the coming of Jesus Christ would be like this: He will return from Heaven with a shout. He will cause the dead in Christ to rise first. He will implement the Rapture of the living saints as they are caught up together with the resurrected dead saints to meet Him in the air. What a moment of triumph when both the resurrection of the Christian dead and living saints takes place! What a translation! All of us who know Jesus Christ as Savior and Lord will be part of that defining moment in time. We all will realize the Lord's presence in a way never known before as we meet Him in the air. Christ's promise to us is residence with Him forever. Where do you want to reside forever?

No wonder Paul would say, "Therefore encourage one another with these words." (1 Thessalonians 4:18). Our blessed hope is first comforting. This is a great word of encouragement! We all need words of encouragement, words that bring healing, words full of mercy. Our God is the God of all comfort and all mercies. Our hope also is purifying (1 John 3:3). One day we will be like Jesus Christ when He is revealed from Heaven. We shall see Him as He is. If you have this hope in you, you purify yourself, just as Jesus is pure.

Finally, it is an activating hope. We are to occupy, do business, and be in service for the King of kings and Lord of lords. Jesus said, "So he called ten of his servants and gave them ten minas. 'Put this money to work,' he said, 'until I come back.'" (Luke 19:13). Who are you expecting? His name is Jesus. Colossians 3:4 says, "When Christ, who is your life, appears, then you also will appear with him in glory." The great trumpeting translation is our blessed hope. See Appendix G for "The Return of Christ—Man's Great Expectation."

Titus 2:13 says, "While we wait for the blessed hope—the appearing of the glory of our great God and Savior, Jesus Christ." Dead saints (whose spirits are now in Heaven and their bodies in the graves) from the day of Pentecost to the day of the Rapture will be resurrected and translated. These are the dead in Christ. Living saints will be translated (no need of resurrection because there is no death for the living saints at the time of the Rapture). These are the alive in Christ. All saints will be translated to meet Christ. Translation means to transfer to another place with a change taking place. *New bodies are promised.* My body is wearing out. It is no longer new! When I receive my new body, what a day that will be! What a day it will be for you, too, as you believe in the saving knowledge of Jesus' death, burial, resurrection, ascension, and one day coming back again; perhaps today? The Lord is coming back. Are we living our lives before God the Father in service for the King of kings and Lord of lords? We have this hope in us, and we purify ourselves even as He is pure. Jesus is altogether lovely, and we are to be lovely, too. We are to be pure as He is pure. We are not to sit idly by. We are to be in service for Christ, even as the signs of the end of the age multiply around us.

Current events in our world dictate that we heed the minor prophet Amos' word, "Therefore this is what I will do to you, Israel, and because I will do this to you, Israel, prepare to meet your God" (Amos 4:12). Current events, signs of the end of the age, and prophetic warnings are converging at the same time in our generation. Certainly, biblical prophecies are being realized as never before in human history. I see a renewed public interest today concerning the end times. Books, movies, and diplomatic relationships between the nations of the world abound with end-time predictions. We are to watch for signs, and when they converge on one generation at one time and place, we can then be sure that we're close to the end of our age. I've shared that the only hope for mankind is salvation found in Jesus Christ alone. It is also true that the great hope of the Christian faith rests in the promised return of Jesus Christ. He will keep His promise. We have seen terrorist attacks, massive storms, increased solar flare activity, climate change, economic decline, intense earthquakes, and tsunamis in our generation. All of these are unprecedented planetary occurrences on the level of apocalyptic proportion. Keep an eye on Israel. She has been under constant barrage of rockets fired into her territory during 2013 and 2014 from terrorists threatening her demise. Even after Israel withdrew from the Gaza Strip in 2005, terrorists continued firing more than 11,000 rockets into Israel. Over 5 million Israelis are currently living under threat of rocket attacks. Hamas and many other radical Islamic Jihad groups are publicly saying, "Israel will be wiped off the map." Because of all these occurrences, I believe the Middle East "War of Gog and Magog" predicted by the major prophet Ezekiel, is ready to unfold at any time. The attack will be against God's chosen people, Israel. The coalition of nations will be led by Russia and Iran (ancient Persia). Let's continue to pray for the peace of Jerusalem. Hear God's promise in Psalm 122:6, "Pray for the peace of Jerusalem: 'May those who love you be secure.'"

I believe it's time to revisit the revival of the 1970s. There were many salvations as the message of Christ's imminent return was preached. We should have the same emphasis today. The prophetical books in the 1970s greatly influenced my thinking about Christ's return, especially *The Late Great Planet Earth,* written by Hal Lindsey. In my heart, I've never doubted that Jesus was coming. The news of the day does not shake my confidence about Jesus Christ, His past, present, and future. He is eternal God. He has always existed. He came to earth to die for our sins. He ascended into Heaven. He is coming back. Let's get the word out. The Bible predicts the unfolding of a great drama of the ages, beginning with Christ's second coming, and ending with the eternal state. These truths are presented in this book. The Holy Spirit of God is unveiling the end times. This Revelation is called the Apocalypse. There is trouble ahead. The warning is clear in Amos 4:12. Be prepared to meet your God. The Lord is at hand (Philippians 4:5). He is near. He will come back. Jesus' very last words He said in the Word of God are of great encouragement, "Yes, I am coming soon" (Revelation 22:20). He is coming quickly. No doctrine is more closely linked to how we live and serve Jesus today in practical daily life than that of His return. Today, Jesus speaks, "Come to me, all you who are weary and burdened, and I will give you rest" (Matthew 11:28). Come to Jesus. The Great Trumpeting Translation could happen today. Ready?

Note: A great resource on the subject matter of this chapter is the work by Jack Van Impe, *Everything You Always Wanted to Know about PROPHECY but Didn't Know Who to Ask!*

THREE

The Great Testing

> By the grace God has given me, I laid a foundation as a wise builder, and someone else is building on it. But each one should build with care. For no one can lay any foundation other than the one already laid, which is Jesus Christ. If anyone builds on this foundation using gold, silver, costly stones, wood, hay or straw, their work will be shown for what it is, because the Day will bring it to light. It will be revealed with fire, and the fire will test the quality of each person's work. If what has been built survives, the builder will receive a reward. If it is burned up, the builder will suffer loss but yet will be saved—even though only as one escaping through the flames. (1 Corinthians 3:10-15)

In the last chapter we saw that the Body of Christ (dead and living saints), at the Rapture, will be ushered into the heavenly state to be with the Lord. At the Rapture, Jesus will come for us to take us with Him to Heaven. After the dead are raised first, and living saints are caught up together with them to meet Jesus in the air, they will be translated and ushered into Heaven.

What God has revealed in His Word, He wants us to understand clearly. The great escape is the Rapture of the Church, but the Church must face judgment. When the Rapture happens, it is like a "spiritual yoyo." Christ comes in the air, and we are taken up with Him. The coming of Christ at the Rapture will be quick in time. He returns for us and we go back with Him to Heaven. What a change of scenery that will be! We will find ourselves standing for the great testing. We will all stand before the Judgment Seat of Christ in God's Throne Room. In the Greek it is called *Bema* and from this one Greek word we have our translation, Judgment Seat. It is the *Bema* of Christ. Paul made many references to athletic competition in the New Testament. It seems that Paul was likely using *Bema* as it applied to Greek sports. The winner of a particular contest (having followed the rules of competition and won) was honored at the *Bema*. There he was crowned with a laurel wreath, not for punishment, but for reward or award.

It is the great testing. It is the next event for the Church after the Rapture. The definition of *Bema* is that judgment of the Church in Heaven in which the believer's deeds in this life are examined by the Lord, and the deeds done in Christ's name will be rewarded. This is a sobering thought for believers. God wants us to have 20/20 vision on our spiritual eye chart. The judgment is answering for what we have done after salvation. We are going to have to go before the judgment. The big question is, does it matter how we live today? Yes, it does. Paul said in Romans 6:1-2, "What shall we say, then? Shall we go on sinning so that grace may increase? By no means! We are those who have died to sin; how can we live in it any longer?" The words "by no means" in the Greek are *me genoito*. God forbid that we continue to sin knowing that God will forgive sin and His grace will increase. We do not have a spiritual license to sin. It means no way should we continue in sin. God's grace forgives our sin. The Church is not a "rest home for saints," but a "hospital for sinners." We still sin. First John 1:9 says, "If we confess our sins, he is faithful and just and will forgive us our sins and purify us from all unrighteousness."

Everything we do after we have been saved will be brought before the Judgment Seat of Christ. The believer's deeds and works will be judged. Not only will our works be judged, but also the motives of our hearts. You may not know my true motive, but God does. He looks not on the outward appearance of man. God looks upon the heart. The *Bema* is technically the official seat of a judge. It is a tribunal, but it's not a judgment center, because associated with this word are the ideas of prominence, dignity, authority, honor, and reward rather than the ideas of judgment and punishment. When God's Word says, "the builder will suffer loss" (1 Corinthians 3:15), it refers to a loss of reward or award. So, it is not punishment. It is not a judgment center. It is a reward center. It is a trophy case center. The meaning of *Bema* is technically an award seat.

The subjects of this judgment are all believers of this age, the Age of Grace, the Age of the Church, the Age of the Holy Spirit. The time of this testing will be after the Rapture in Heaven and during the Tribulation hour on earth. Just think about the Church not being here during the Tribulation Period. Revelation, chapters six through eighteen, reveal the seven-year Tribulation on the earth. The Church is never mentioned. Why? We are not on the earth. We are in Heaven during this time period standing before the judgment seat of Christ. Paul says in Romans 14:7-12,

> For none of us lives for ourselves alone, and none of us dies for ourselves alone. If we live, we live for the Lord; and if we die, we die for the Lord. So, whether we live or die, we belong to the Lord. For this very reason, Christ died and returned to life so that he might be the Lord of both the dead and the living. You, then, why do you judge your brother or sister? Or why do you treat them with contempt? For we will all stand before God's judgment seat. It is written: "As surely as I live," says the Lord, "every knee will bow before me; every tongue will acknowledge God." So then, each of us will give an account of ourselves to God.

Paul is writing to believers. He is writing to the church at Rome. The judgment seat of Christ is the *Bema*. *All* here does not mean everyone who has ever lived. *All* means *all* believers (Romans 14:10). That is the context; only believers will give an account before God. I do not have to give an account for you, and you do not have to give an account for me. We have to give an account before the Lord at this judgment seat. Who are the participants? The ones participating are *all* believers of this age, the Church Age. Paul again says in 2 Corinthians 5:6-10,

> Therefore we are always confident and know that as long as we are at home in the body we are away from the Lord. For we live by faith, not by sight. We are confident, I say, and would prefer to be away from the body and at home with the Lord. So we make it our goal to please him, whether we are at home in the body or away from it. For we must all appear before the judgment seat of Christ, so that each of us may receive what is due us for the things done while in the body, whether good or bad.

This is what Paul said to the church at Corinth. God will judge us on the basis of things we have done in this life after salvation. We will receive the things done in the body, whether good or bad. The judgment is solely based on what's done in the body. We will all appear before Christ in judgment. The word appear in the Greek is *phaneroo*. It means to be manifested, to declare, to be readily perceived, or to be rendered apparent. On that day you will fully know. Those around you will fully know. The Lord already fully knows. The day will declare it, bring it to light. Not only will we fully know, but we will also know our deeds, good or bad.

The word bad in the Greek is *kakos*. It means that which is worthless or good for nothing. It also can be translated improperly motivated. *Kakos* is works that are improperly motivated. The Lord knows the thoughts and intentions of our hearts. After we are saved, we do works. The Bible teaches in Ephesians 2:8-10, "For it is by grace you have been saved, through faith—and this is not from yourselves, it is the gift of God—not by works, so that no one can boast. For we are God's handiwork, created in Christ Jesus to do good works, which God prepared in advance for us to do." Those works of the believer are going to be judged. What we do for the Lord Jesus that brings glory to Him will result in our receiving gold, silver, and precious stones. What we do to glorify self, we will receive wood, hay, and straw. These works are improperly motivated. These will be burned up. We are going to be judged and receive the things due us, awards (rewards) for the things done while in our earthly bodies, whether they are good or worthless.

What does 2 Corinthians 5:10 say about the Judge? The Judge is Christ. John 5:22-27 says,

> Moreover, the Father judges no one, but has entrusted all judgment to the Son, that all may honor the Son just as they honor the Father. Whoever does not honor the Son does not honor the Father, who sent him. Very truly I tell you, whoever hears my word and believes him who sent me has eternal life and will not be judged, but has crossed over from death to life. Very truly I tell you, a time is coming and has now come when the dead will hear the voice of the Son of God and those who hear will live. For as the Father has life in himself, so he has granted the Son also to have life in himself. And he has given him authority to judge because he is the Son of Man.

Believer, remember what Jesus Christ has done for you and me. Let's glorify Him in our works, for one day we will stand before Him in judgment.

Now, what is the nature of the judgment? What is the issue at hand? What will be examined? What is the purpose? The judgment is not for salvation, not to judge my sins, but a true manifestation of the believer's deeds. Remember "appear" means to be made manifest, readily perceived, whether useless or worthwhile. Jesus said in Matthew 10:26-27, "So do not be afraid of them, for there is nothing concealed that will not be disclosed, or hidden that will not be made known. What I tell you in the dark, speak in the daylight; what is whispered in your ear, proclaim from the roofs." Also, we see how clearly Paul states this truth in 1 Corinthians 4:5: "Therefore judge nothing before the appointed time; wait until the Lord comes. He will bring to light what is hidden in darkness and will expose the motives of the heart. At that time each will receive their praise from God." Praise from God will be given at the Judgment Seat of Christ.

The method of examination of our works will be by fire. It is the eternal, infinite, searching gaze of Jesus. The eyes of Jesus Christ will be like a blazing fire. Literally, things will be turned inside out. The author of Hebrews says in Hebrews 4:12-13,

> For the word of God is alive and active. Sharper than any double-edged sword, it penetrates even to dividing soul and spirit, joints and marrow; it judges the thoughts and attitudes of the heart. Nothing in all creation is hidden from God's sight. Everything is uncovered and laid bare before the eyes of him to whom we must give account.

Believers will give an account at the *Bema* of Christ.

What will be the result? Christ's judgment will test the character and quality of our works. You talk about quality control! They are either *rejected* or *accepted*. Will they be gold, silver, and precious stones to be accepted by Christ, or wood, hay, and straw to be rejected by Christ? The result will determine our rewards.

What are the rewards associated with Resurrection and Rapture? Jesus spoke of the Resurrection this way in Luke 14:12-14,

> When you give a luncheon or dinner, do not invite your friends, your brothers or sisters, your relatives, or your rich neighbors; if you do, they may invite you back and so you will be repaid. But when you give a banquet, invite the poor, the crippled, the lame, the blind, and you will be blessed. Although they cannot repay you, you will be repaid at the resurrection of the righteous.

Paul follows up in 2 Timothy 4:1-2, "In the presence of God and of Christ Jesus, who will judge the living and the dead, and in view of his appearing and his kingdom, I give you this charge: Preach the word; be prepared in season and out of season; correct, rebuke and encourage—with great patience and careful instruction." He says later in the chapter in verse 8, "Now there is in store for me the crown of righteousness, which the Lord, the righteous Judge, will award to me on that day—and not only to me, but also to all who have longed for his appearing." There are rewards associated with Resurrection and Rapture.

Now let's look at the rewards associated with the great testing, the *Bema* of Jesus Christ. The New Testament mentions five crowns. The first crown is the imperishable (incorruptible) crown. 1 Corinthians 9:25-27 says,

> Everyone who competes in the games goes into strict training. They do it to get a crown that will not last, but we do it to get a crown that will last forever. Therefore I do not run like someone running aimlessly; I do not fight like a boxer beating the air. No, I strike a blow to my body and make it my slave so that after I have preached to others, I myself will not be disqualified for the prize.

The second crown is the crown of rejoicing found in 1 Thessalonians 2:19, "For what is our hope, our joy, or the crown in which we will glory in the presence of our Lord Jesus when he comes? Is it not you?" See John 4:36 and Daniel 12:3.

The third crown is mentioned by James. It is the crown of life or martyr's crown in James 1:12, "Blessed is the one who perseveres under trial because, having stood the test, that person will receive the crown of life that the Lord has promised to those who love him." See also Revelation 2:10.

The fourth crown named is the crown of righteousness found in 2 Timothy 4:8, "Now there is in store for me the crown of righteousness, which the Lord, the righteous Judge, will award to me on that day — and not only to me, but also to all who have longed for his appearing." I love this crown. I love and long for Christ's appearing! Do you?

The fifth crown is the crown of glory or the service crown shown in 1 Peter 5:4, "And when the Chief Shepherd appears, you will receive the crown of glory that will never fade away." See John 17:17.

The key point to make here is that we are earning the crowns now! Use your spiritual gift(s) to glorify God. Judgment and reward are waiting. See Appendix H, Spiritual Gifts, Rewards, and Judgment for an extensive outline study on the five crowns found in the New Testament.

Before we move on to a new chapter on the Great Tribulation, let's look briefly at two events that will take place after we are judged. First is the Marriage of the Lamb. It is that event in which the Church will be eternally united to Jesus Christ, the Bridegroom (2 Corinthians 11:1-3; Revelation 19:6-8). After that glorious occasion, we will celebrate the Marriage Feast of the Lamb. This feast includes Israel. Old Testament saints and Tribulation saints are all summoned to this Supper (Revelation 19:9). Several parables given by Jesus reveal this glorious event: the Parable of the Wedding Banquet found in Matthew 22:1-14, the Parable of the Ten Virgins found in Matthew 25:1-13, and the Parable of the Great Banquet found in Luke 14:15-24.

Study the following on The Marriage of the Lamb and The Marriage Feast:

The Marriage of the Lamb

Definition: That event which takes place in Heaven in which the Church, the Bride of Christ, is eternally united to Christ, the Bridegroom.
Time: After the Rapture and the Judgment Seat of Christ (for service) and before the Second Advent or the Revelation of Christ.
Place: In Heaven.
Participants: Christ and the Church of Jesus Christ (marriage union).
Scripture: (John 3:29; Romans 7:4; 2 Corinthians 11:3).
Espoused: Means to fit together, to join in relationship, presented in one group or body to Christ.
Proof: The Church, all born again believers = the Bride.
Christ is the Bridegroom and the Church is symbolized as the Bride (Ephesians 5:21-27; Revelation 19:6-8).
Details: Dressed or clothed in fine, white linen, bright, and clean.
Significance: The Church's union with Christ has been completed.

Again, see Appendix D for a complete explanation of *Behold the Bridegroom Comes,* by Renald Showers.

The Marriage Feast or the Marriage Supper: Party! The Big Bash!

The Old Testament saints and the Tribulation saints are summoned to this great feast.

Matthew 22:1-14 speaks of the Parable of the Wedding Banquet. Includes Israel!

Luke 14:15-24 speaks of the Parable of the Great Banquet.

Matthew 25:1-13 speaks of the Parable of the Ten Virgins (parabolic or symbolic picture of the Millennium). See Matthew 24:36-51; Revelation 19:7-14.

They honor Christ and the Bride.

Reason: The completion of God's work in the Church of Jesus Christ!

The Marriage of the Lamb will be a great event happening in Heaven after we have stood before The Judgment Seat of Christ (Bema). The Marriage Feast/Supper will be a great event happening on earth after the Bema and The Marriage of the Lamb, and after we come back with Jesus Christ (Revelation 19) to the earth. Praise the Lord!

Now we move to the Great Tribulation.

Note: A great resource on the subject matter of this chapter is David Jeremiah's work, *Escape the Coming Night*.

FOUR

The Great Tribulation

Seventy "sevens" are decreed for your people and your holy city to finish transgression, to put an end to sin, to atone for wickedness, to bring in everlasting righteousness, to seal up vision and prophecy and to anoint the Most Holy Place. Know and understand this: From the time the word goes out to restore and rebuild Jerusalem until the Anointed One, the ruler, comes, there will be seven "sevens," and sixty-two "sevens." It will be rebuilt with streets and a trench, but in times of trouble. After the sixty-two "sevens," the Anointed One will be put to death and will have nothing. The people of the ruler who will come will destroy the city and the sanctuary. The end will come like a flood: War will continue until the end, and desolations have been decreed. He will confirm a covenant with many for one "seven." In the middle of the "seven" he will put an end to sacrifice and offering. And at the temple he will set up an abomination that causes desolation, until the end that is decreed is poured out on him. (Daniel 9:24-27)

The Tribulation hour is the seven year world-wide judgment that is the seventieth week of Daniel in which God brings to an end the Times of the Gentiles, prepares the nation of Israel for her Messiah, and pours out His judgment on unbelieving men and nations. All who are left upon the earth at the Rapture will enter the hour of Tribulation. I would like to go to the Word of God for the definition and description of this period. First, in Isaiah 26:20-21, the prophet records,

> Go, my people, enter your rooms and shut the doors behind you; hide yourselves for a little while until his wrath has passed by. See, the LORD is coming out of his dwelling to punish the people of the earth for their sins. The earth will disclose the blood shed on it; the earth will conceal its slain no longer.

The Tribulation is called the indignation (Daniel 8:19 KJV), God's wrath. Second, in Jeremiah 30:7-9, the prophet records,

> How awful that day will be! No other will be like it. It will be a time of trouble for Jacob, but he will be saved out of it. "In that day," declares the LORD Almighty, "I will break the yoke off their necks and will tear off their bonds; no longer will foreigners enslave them. Instead, they will serve the LORD their God and David their king, whom I will raise up for them."

Third, in Daniel 12:1-2, the prophet records,

> At that time Michael, the great prince who protects your people, will arise. There will be a time of distress such as has not happened from the beginning of nations until then. But at that time your people—everyone whose name is found written in the book—will be delivered. Multitudes who sleep in the dust of the earth will awake: some to everlasting life, others to shame and everlasting contempt.

Look at this description. It is truly the time of trouble for Jacob, for the nation of Israel, Daniel's people. It will be an awful time. It is a time when God's wrath is poured out. Michael, the Archangel for the nation of Israel, is Israel's guardian angel. He is the great prince who protects Daniel's people. Daniel's people are the Jews. In Daniel 10:13, he is called "one of the chief princes." In Daniel 10:21, he is called "Michael, your prince." Michael is mentioned twice in the New Testament. Jude 1:9 says, "But even the archangel Michael, when he was disputing with the devil about the body of Moses, did not himself dare to condemn him for slander but said, 'The Lord rebuke you!'" The last time *Michael* is mentioned is in the Book of Revelation, chapter twelve, verse seven, "Then war broke out in heaven. Michael and his angels fought against the dragon, and the dragon and his angels fought back." *Michael* the Archangel, and his angels win the war in Heaven at the midpoint of the Tribulation. Amen!

God is going to preserve and deliver the nation of Israel out of the great Tribulation hour. Paul reveals in Romans, chapters 9-11, that God still has a grand and glorious plan for His chosen people, Israel. Paul anguishes over his people in Romans 9:1-5:

> I speak the truth in Christ—I am not lying, my conscience confirms it through the Holy Spirit—I have great sorrow and unceasing anguish in my heart. For I could wish that I myself were cursed and cut off from Christ for the sake of my people, those of my own race, the people of Israel. Theirs is the adoption to sonship; theirs the divine glory, the covenants, the receiving of the law, the temple worship and the promises. Theirs are the patriarchs, and from them is traced the human ancestry of the Messiah, who is God over all, forever praised! Amen.

God has not rejected His chosen people forever! God will give them a future. God will give hope. However, they still must endure the Tribulation where there will be a time of distress and trouble not seen like it since the beginning of nations.

Jesus gave the same thought in Matthew 24:21-22, "For then there will be great distress, unequaled from the beginning of the world until now—and never to be equaled again. If those days had not been cut short, no one would survive, but for the sake of the elect those days will be shortened." There has never been a time of persecution, trouble, and distress like this period of time. So after this period of time, there will never be a time equal to it again in human history. Today, in current events, in our world there are periods of persecution, trouble, and distress, but none will equal this coming day of wrath for seven years on the earth. All who are left upon the earth at the time of the Rapture will enter the Tribulation. Jesus spoke of wars and rumors of wars. Wars and rumors of wars are constant today. Jesus spoke of another period of time of great Tribulation such as has not been since the beginning of the world until this time. There has never been and never will be after the seven years are over, a period of time like this. God has shortened those days for the sake of His elect. Praise God, it is only seven years. Who could survive longer than that? When we think of the twenty-one judgments in the Book of Revelation, we have to ask ourselves, "How many can survive these judgments, especially when hailstones weighing one hundred pounds start falling at the end of the Tribulation?"

Luke 21:20-28 reveals,

> When you see Jerusalem being surrounded by armies, you will know that its desolation is near. Then let those who are in Judea flee to the mountains, let those in the city get out, and let those in the country not enter the city. For this is the time of punishment in fulfillment of all that has been written. How dreadful it will be in those days for pregnant women and nursing mothers! There will be great distress in the land and wrath against this people. They will fall by the sword and will be taken as prisoners to all the nations. Jerusalem will be trampled on by the Gentiles until the times of the Gentiles are fulfilled. There will be signs in the sun, moon and stars. On the earth, nations will be in anguish and perplexity at the roaring and tossing of the sea. People will faint from terror, apprehensive of what is coming on the world, for the heavenly bodies will be shaken. At that time, they will see the Son of Man coming in a cloud with power and great glory.

> When these things begin to take place, stand up and lift
> up your heads, because your redemption is drawing near.

We're told that the Times of the Gentiles will not end until Jerusalem is no longer ruled by other nations. But when will this domination and interference finally end? Perhaps it will be when Israel receives undisputed sovereignty over Jerusalem and the Temple Mount. Luke 21:24 is the only place where the Times of the Gentiles are mentioned by name. Jesus is speaking. "They will fall by the sword and will be taken as prisoners to all the nations. Jerusalem will be trampled on by the Gentiles until the times of the Gentiles are fulfilled" (Luke 21:24). Jesus speaks in the plural, "the times of the Gentiles are fulfilled" (Luke 21:24).

Revelation 11:2 gives us another truth about the Times of the Gentiles. It says, "But exclude the outer court; do not measure it, because it has been given to the Gentiles. They will trample on the holy city for 42 months." So we see clearly that the Times of the Gentiles trampling Jerusalem (as defined by Luke 21:24) is not over until the last forty-two months of the Great Tribulation are finished, the last three and one-half years. This, by the way, is the same point at which the seventieth week of Daniel ends. So, the Times of the Gentiles is that time period from the dominion of the Babylonian Empire under King Nebuchadnezzar over Israel in 605 B.C. until the end of the Great Tribulation. King Nebuchadnezzar and his vast armies successfully conquered Jerusalem. That period of time is extended in which the land given in covenant (Abrahamic and Palestinian Covenants) by God to Abraham and his descendants is occupied by the Gentiles. The Davidic throne (Davidic Covenant) is empty of any legal heir in the lineage of David, and it will continue until the Messiah returns at the great triumph seen in the next chapter (Revelation 19). Israel is given a new heart promised by the New Covenant. At His return (the Revelation), Christ will subdue the nations, He will end the Great Tribulation at the key battle of Armageddon (Revelation 16:16), deliver the land of Israel from its Gentile occupants, and bring the nation Israel into her covenanted blessings in the Millennium (see chapter 6, The Great Ten Centuries).

It is true that many times in Scripture that prophecy has a double fulfillment, a near and distant fulfillment. In A.D. 70, Titus, the Roman General destroyed Jerusalem and Herod's Temple. This will be another time when Jerusalem will be destroyed. This is a time of punishment and of days of vengeance so that all things about this time may be fulfilled. One day, God will have His say, His way, and His day. So much has been written about this seven-year Tribulation period in both Testaments. It will be a time of fulfillment. Remember earlier when we looked at prophecy, I said prophecy was God's revelation of future events and things? It is a lamp shining in a dark place, and it is God's history, written in advance. It is God's description of things. It is written from God's perspective. About half of prophecy concerning Jesus Christ has been fulfilled, but the other half still awaits fulfillment. The first half was fulfilled literally, and I believe the last will also be fulfilled literally. Jesus said how dreadful it will be in that day. There will be great distress in the land of Israel and wrath upon the nation of Israel. It is the time of Jacob's trouble.

Israel will be led away captive into other nations, and Jerusalem will be trampled by the Gentiles until the Times of the Gentiles are brought to pass. Israel is in the Land promised her today, even though she does not enjoy the full extent and boundary of the Land promised her by God. Israel is not forever in the Land today, not permanently in the Land today. There will be another dispersion or Diaspora, a scattering of God's chosen people. Jesus spoke of this during His public ministry (Matthew 24:15-21). The "abomination of desolation," spoken of through the prophet Daniel will be set up by the False Prophet on behalf of the Beast at the midpoint of the Tribulation. "He will oppose and will exalt himself over everything that is called God or is worshiped, so that he sets himself up in God's temple, proclaiming himself to be God" (2 Thessalonians 2:4). "Because of the signs it was given power to perform on behalf of the first beast, it deceived the inhabitants of the earth. It ordered them to set up an image in honor of the beast who was wounded by the sword and yet lived" (Revelation 13:14). Jesus tells those living in the generation of the Great Tribulation to flee Judea at that time, and He speaks of the flight being difficult in several situations. Read Matthew 24. Jesus says when He comes at the great triumph

(Revelation 19), the elect will be gathered back to Israel. This takes place at the end of the Great Tribulation.

> Then will appear the sign of the Son of Man in heaven. And then all the peoples of the earth will mourn when they see the Son of Man coming on the clouds of heaven, with power and great glory. And he will send his angels with a loud trumpet call, and they will gather his elect from the four winds, from one end of the heavens to the other. (Matthew 24:30-31)

The leaders of the nation of Israel, today, have started reading and believing the prophecies of the Old Testament where it refers to Israel never being uprooted from the land again. One verse Netanyahu quoted when he addressed the United Nations on October 1, 2013, was, "'I will plant Israel in their own land, never again to be uprooted from the land I have given them,' says the LORD your God" (Amos 9:15). I can see why a Jewish person today would say that prophecy is fulfilled. Their eyes are blinded to the truths of the New Testament. Jesus is God. Jesus is Jehovah. On earth, Jesus spoke volumes of prophecies concerning the nation of Israel. Israel is not now permanently in the land. She will be, in the future, only after these seven years of tribulation. Yes, something wonderful happened in our generation. On May 14, 1948, Israel was reborn as a nation. Prophecy was fulfilled as Isaiah foretold in Isaiah 66:8, "Who has ever heard of such things? Who has ever seen things like this? Can a country be born in a day or a nation be brought forth in a moment? Yet no sooner is Zion in labor than she gives birth to her children." Ezekiel chapters 36 and 37 were fulfilled.

So, the believing Jew or Gentile today reads Matthew, chapters 24 and 25, and understands there will be the Great Tribulation for Israel. She must flee her homeland again, but God will gather her from the nations for the final time, and Amos 9:15 will come to pass. An unbelieving Jew (one who does not believe Jesus Christ is the Son of God, the Messiah, the Anointed One of God who died on Calvary for the sins of Jews and Gentiles), in these terms, would see Amos 9:15 as fulfilled on May 14, 1948. From the lens of the

New Testament, though, it is not yet at the present time, but Amos 9:15 will be fulfilled at the end of the Great Tribulation and during the great ten centuries (the Millennium) when she will never be uprooted from the land God has given her *ever again*!

In the future, Israel will dwell permanently in the land when Jesus Christ, the King of kings and Lord of lords, will return at the end of the Tribulation hour to fight against His people's enemies. Israel will enjoy the land for one thousand years, called the Millennium. We will look at the Millennium in a future chapter.

Now, let's look at Revelation 11:1-8:

> I was given a reed like a measuring rod and was told, "Go and measure the temple of God and the altar, with its worshipers. But exclude the outer court; do not measure it, because it has been given to the Gentiles. They will trample on the holy city for 42 months. And I will appoint my two witnesses, and they will prophesy for 1,260 days, clothed in sackcloth." They are "the two olive trees" and the two lampstands, and "they stand before the Lord of the earth." If anyone tries to harm them, fire comes from their mouths and devours their enemies. This is how anyone who wants to harm them must die. They have power to shut up the heavens so that it will not rain during the time they are prophesying, and they have power to turn the waters into blood and to strike the earth with every kind of plague as often as they want. Now when they have finished their testimony, the beast that comes up from the Abyss will attack them, and overpower and kill them. Their bodies will lie in the public square of the great city—which is figuratively called Sodom and Egypt—where also their Lord was crucified.

These are the two witnesses at the end of the Tribulation hour. They will prophesy for three and a half years. The Antichrist will kill them and their dead bodies will lie in the street (the main street or the public square) of Jerusalem (Revelation 11:8). Jerusalem at that time is described as Sodom and Egypt. Sodom and Egypt represent the world system of sin under the dominion of Satan. Jerusalem is literal, but she is spiritually called by these terms. Jerusalem is where our Lord Jesus Christ was crucified. If the allegorist wants all of Revelation to be symbolic or allegory, he would have a difficult time here interpreting this passage other than Jerusalem where our Lord Jesus Christ was crucified. Jerusalem is literal. The crucifixion of Jesus is literal. The two prophets (witnesses) who prophesy during the last half of The Great Tribulation are literal. Literal, literal, literal! The Tribulation will be a literal period of time. All who are left upon the earth at the Rapture will enter the Great Tribulation. The Tribulation is not mere chastisement or suffering; it is the outpouring of God's wrath upon rebellious man, though He may use human agencies like the Beast and the False Prophet. The two witnesses are resurrected by God and will ascend into Heaven. Jesus is coming at the Revelation at the end of the seven years of the Great Tribulation. We will look at the Second Coming of Christ (the Revelation) in another chapter.

Let's look at a quick overview of the Tribulation hour. The Day of the Lord begins. The Day of Christ is the Day of the Rapture. Paul said in 2 Thessalonians 2:1-4,

> Concerning the coming of our Lord Jesus Christ and our being gathered to him, we ask you, brothers and sisters, not to become easily unsettled or alarmed by the teaching allegedly from us—whether by a prophecy or by word of mouth or by letter—asserting that the day of the Lord has already come. Don't let anyone deceive you in any way, for that day will not come until the rebellion occurs and the man of lawlessness is revealed, the man doomed to destruction. He will oppose and will exalt himself over everything that is called God or is worshiped, so that he sets himself up in God's temple, proclaiming himself to be God.

The Day of Lord begins after the Rapture. It is the day of doom, gloom, darkness, and distress pictured in the Old Testament. It is a day of wrath and indignation.

The Antichrist will be the ruler who establishes a covenant with Israel and the nations of the world. The peace treaty will be ratified. This man is going to be a "diplomat of diplomats." He is going to be a "golden-tongued orator." He is going to be a "military genius." He will be "the incarnation of Satan" on the planet Earth, and as such, will be given world control. He will covet world supremacy, and then he attains it. His leadership will be unquestioned. He will be a world hero. He is going to do something that no one else has ever done. He will solve the Middle East conflict. A peace treaty will be ratified between Israel and the nations of the world. Daniel 9:24-27 speaks loudly and clearly here. Read Daniel, chapters 9-12, for an in-depth look at the Antichrist and the period of time he will be given or granted to rule by the authority of God. He could do nothing unless it was allowed by God. He will be "given power to take peace from the earth" as seen in Revelation 6:4. Satan's power, authority, and time are also limited. Satan "knows that his time is short" (Revelation 12:12).

The warning of Scripture must be heeded here. First Thessalonians 5:3 reads, "While people are saying, 'Peace and safety,' destruction will come on them suddenly, as labor pains on a pregnant woman, and they will not escape." The prophets concur, "'Peace, peace,' they say, when there is no peace" (Jeremiah 6:14; 8:11; Ezekiel 13:10; 13:16). Even though the Antichrist will solve the Middle East conflict, it is only an illusion of true peace. Israel will be deceived.

Next, in the overview, the religious multitudes who missed the Rapture will merge into the one world apostate church. At the Rapture, the true Church of Jesus Christ is evacuated. We are in Heaven at the Judgment Seat of Christ. The organized religious system is left on the earth after the Rapture. Religion is man seeking God. Christianity is God seeking man in His Son, Jesus Christ. The apostate church is described in the Book of Revelation as the Great Prostitute (Revelation 17). This Great Prostitute will sit on the Beast for three and a half years until the Antichrist destroys the false church in Revelation 18:10. It says, "Terrified at her torment, they will stand far off and cry: 'Woe! Woe to you, great city, you mighty city of Babylon! In one hour your doom has come!'" When the Tribulation Period starts, this apostate church, this super church is going to be in existence. The Antichrist comes on the scene, being very religious. He tolerates the organized church. He even makes a peace treaty with Israel, and Israel is allowed to start religious activities in the rebuilt Temple. Israel will again start sacrificing to Jehovah God. She will offer the prescribed daily, monthly, and seasonal sacrifices. She will continue three and one-half years until the Antichrist breaks his treaty with Israel at the midpoint of the Great Tribulation.

The Beast will use religion. The Beast and the kingdom of the Beast will be a religious system, a political system, an economic system, and a commercial system pictured in the Book of Revelation, especially in chapters 17 and 18. This apostate church is pictured as riding on top of the Beast, influencing the Beast. Then at the midpoint of the Tribulation hour when the Beast goes into the Temple and proclaims himself as God, He will at that time destroy the apostate church (2 Thessalonians 2:1-4). So, at the Rapture, the religious multitudes merge into the one world apostate church, and at this point the ecumenical movement is a success.

A time of great prosperity comes to the nations under the Antichrist. He will use bribery and flattery and the economy will prosper during the first half of the Tribulation period. The first half will be mild tribulation in which there will be a pseudo peace. We see this in Daniel 8:23-25:

> In the latter part of their reign, when rebels have become completely wicked, a fierce-looking king, a master of intrigue, will arise. He will become very strong, but not by his own power. He will cause astounding devastation and will succeed in whatever he does. He will destroy those who are mighty and the holy people. He will cause deceit to prosper, and he will consider himself superior. When they feel secure, he will destroy many and take his stand against the Prince of princes (Jesus Christ). Yet he will be destroyed, but not by human power.

Also, at the start of the Tribulation Period, Israel believes that peace has come at long last and she reconstructs the Temple. There is an unsettling, uneasy calm; the nation of Israel has been fooled. The nations of the world are deceived, and shortly the Beast will play his "trump card." He is a great deceiver, the great counterfeiter. So the nation of Israel, thinking that peace has come at long last, reconstructs the Temple on its original site. The Beast probably will help in that enterprise. Sacrifices will start again at the Temple site which comprises about thirty-five acres next to the Wailing Wall in Jerusalem (on the Temple Mount). Jerusalem is the only place where Israel can build the Temple, and she will in the future. She is hard at work today with plans, materials, and consensus of popular opinion to do so. Hear what Paul said in 1 Thessalonians 5:1-3: "Now, brothers and sisters, about times and dates we do not need to write to you, for you know very well that the day of the Lord will come like a thief in the night. While people are saying, 'Peace and safety,' destruction will come on them suddenly, as labor pains on a pregnant woman, and they will not escape." On that day they will say there is peace and there is safety. Nothing could be further from the truth.

With the use of computers, the Beast will control every person on the globe. You remember the numbering system, *666;* six is the number for man. The False Prophet causes everyone to worship the Beast. He makes everyone receive the mark of the Beast in his forehead or hand. Those who do not receive the mark of the Beast can neither buy nor sell. In our year 2014, many are saying in the future there will be a cashless society. I believe this is a precursor of what it will look like in the Tribulation. Many are forced to destruction and persecuted for refusing to take the mark of the Beast. It will be a numbering system. Advancement in technology is amazing today. You can hold the world in the palm of your hand. Through global positioning, you can be tracked. You and your family, your business, and livelihood will be under scrutiny of the Beast. It will be very scary.

There arises a False Prophet who causes the multitudes to worship the Beast. In Revelation 13:11-12, it says that this man comes out of the earth (land). The Beast in Revelation 13:1 is pictured as coming out of the sea. Sea is symbolic in Scripture as referring to the nations, the masses of people, the Gentiles. That is why we believe the Beast will be a Gentile, but more than that, in Daniel 9, it speaks of him coming from the Revived Roman Empire, the Western Confederation of Nations. Land in Scripture is symbolic of the nation of Israel. Israel is promised the Land in the Abrahamic and Palestinian covenants. Could this person called the False Prophet be Jewish? Some believe he may even come from the tribe of Dan. I am not sure about that myself. The False Prophet causes the world to worship the Beast and the Image of the Beast.

The Temple is finished; sacrifices are again in practice, and the Beast arrives in Jerusalem. It seems his headquarters during the first three and a half years have been in Rome, Italy. The city is pictured as having seven hills (mountains). Revelation 17:9 says, "This calls for a mind with wisdom. The seven heads are seven hills on which the woman sits." The Beast comes to Jerusalem and plays his trump card.

The Jews are betrayed as the Beast defiles the Holy of Holies in the Temple. Daniel 12:11 says, "From the time that the daily sacrifice is abolished and the abomination that causes desolation is set up, there will be 1,290 days." Daniel further speaks in chapter eleven, verse thirty-one, "His armed forces will rise up to desecrate the temple fortress and will abolish the daily sacrifice. Then they will set up the abomination that causes desolation." Revelation 13:13-14 also speaks loudly,

> And it performed great signs, even causing fire to come down from heaven to the earth in full view of the people. Because of the signs it was given power to perform on behalf of the first beast, it deceived the inhabitants of the earth. It ordered them to set up an image in honor of the beast who was wounded by the sword and yet lived.

"It" here refers to the second Beast, the False Prophet. The image of the Beast seems to be an idol or statue. The False Prophet gives breath to the image. The world is commanded to worship this idol under penalty of being beheaded. However, could the image also be a computer? Just a thought!

Jesus speaks of this time in Matthew 24:15-22. What happens is the image of the Beast is set up in the Holy of Holies in the Temple.

It will be the "abomination of desolation." The "elect" are the Tribulation saints. I believe if God does not shorten the days, no one could survive. The Holy of Holies is desecrated. The False Prophet gives life and breath to this image, and causes the whole world to worship the Beast and his image. Revelation 13:15 says, "The second beast was given power to give breath to the image of the first beast, so that the image could speak and cause all who refused to worship the image to be killed." An in-depth reading of 2 Thessalonians 2:1-17 would be helpful here.

At the beginning of the Great Tribulation, the 144,000 Jewish servants are sealed by God to go forth and preach the Gospel of the Kingdom. The 144,000 are mentioned in the Apocalypse of Jesus called the Book of Revelation in chapter 7. They were not in the Rapture. God seals them with His redemption. The sealed of Israel are mentioned in verse four. To the student of God's Word, if the literal sense makes good sense, look for no other sense. Take God's Word for what it says! It reads, "Then I heard the number of those who were sealed: 144,000 from all the tribes of Israel" (Revelation 7:4). The 144,000 are the true witnesses to Jehovah's power and presence during the Tribulation hour. Please do not confuse the 144,000 in Revelation 7 with the present-day cult that claims to be the true Jehovah's Witnesses. During the Great Tribulation, the 144,000 sealed by God Himself will be the true Jehovah's Witnesses. There is such a great contrast between what one cult teaches today and what God's Word teaches in Revelation 7. I go with God's Word.

Revelation 7:9-17 speaks of a great multitude saved out of this time. In the context, those sealed by God witness to the world and a great multitude, which no one could number, of all nations, tribes, peoples, and tongues, and they are redeemed (Revelation 7:9). The wicked get their seal of 666 in Revelation 13:17-18 under the super-deceiver, the great imitator, the Antichrist. The 144,000 genuine believers in chapter 7 of Revelation during the Tribulation Period receive their seal from the angel of God. The seal is principally a guarantee of ownership and security. The 144,000 cannot be the Church, for the Church is already in Heaven. Here we have Jews with Jewish names to head up Jewish tribes in a Jewish nation called Israel. The 144,000 Jewish servants are anointed by the Holy Spirit

(Joel 2:28-29). These verses describe the situation as these Spirit-filled servants of God proclaim the gospel of the kingdom.

The message of the 144,000 centers on the person and work of Jesus (Acts 10:43). They preach the message of His shed blood and proclaim the advent of the King (Matthew 24:14). This advent is the Revelation or revealing of Christ as King (Revelation 19:16). Again, who are the 144,000? They are 144,000 Jewish "Billy Grahams" sealed by the Spirit of God and preaching the good news of Jesus Christ for the age and dispensation the Tribulation period that will last seven years. You will find this in Revelation 7:1-8. Jesus said in Matthew 24:14, "And this gospel of the kingdom will be preached in the whole world as a testimony to all nations, and then the end will come." Think about 144,000 "Billy Grahams" loosed on the world. It will be a time of great salvation. These are Jewish witnesses, and they will speak about the commandments of the Lord Jesus Christ and the Word of God. Billy Graham celebrated his ninety-fifty birthday in November of 2013. His national message was "My Hope America." His message is the same after decades of preaching. Jesus Christ is our only *hope*. Let's hear the words of 2 Corinthians 6:2, "For he says, 'In the time of my favor I heard you, and in the day of salvation I helped you.' I tell you, now is the time of God's favor, now is the day of salvation."

There will be much salvation during the Tribulation hour, both of Jew and of Gentile. Many will be martyred and persecuted, and their souls are pictured underneath God's altar in Heaven in Revelation 6:9-11:

> When he opened the fifth seal, I saw under the altar the souls of those who had been slain because of the word of God and the testimony they had maintained. They called out in a loud voice, "How long, Sovereign Lord, holy and true, until you judge the inhabitants of the earth and avenge our blood?" Then each of them was given a white robe, and they were told to wait a little longer, until the full number of their fellow servants, their brothers and sisters, were killed just as they had been.

Here is the fifth seal opened by Jesus Christ and it reveals the cry of the martyrs during the Tribulation hour. Many will be saved, but many also will be persecuted to death. Some will make it through these awful seven years, and will enter into the Millennium Kingdom in bodies like we have today, in mortal bodies.

Jesus Himself says in Matthew 24:13, "But the one who stands firm to the end will be saved." It is the one who endures to the end. It is not only a spiritual salvation, but a physical preservation during the worst seven years of human history. It will never be equaled again, nor has it ever happened in our world like it will be during these seven years of tribulation and desolation. Martyrdom for so many is now the price their salvation will cost. They will give their lives in witness for Jesus Christ. Revelation 20:4 says,

> I saw thrones on which were seated those who had been given authority to judge. And I saw the souls of those who had been beheaded because of their testimony about Jesus and because of the word of God. They had not worshiped the beast or its image and had not received its mark on their foreheads or their hands. They came to life and reigned with Christ a thousand years.

A more detailed description is found in Revelation chapter seven. Read now verse nine through verse seventeen.

> After this I looked, and there before me was a great multitude that no one could count, from every nation, tribe, people and language, standing before the throne and before the Lamb. They were wearing white robes and were holding palm branches in their hands. And they cried out in a loud voice: "Salvation belongs to our God, who sits on the throne, and to the Lamb." All the angels were standing around the throne and around the elders and the four living creatures. They fell down on their faces before the throne and worshiped God, saying: "Amen! Praise and glory and wisdom and thanks and honor and power and strength be to our God for ever and ever.

Amen!" Then one of the elders asked me, "These in white robes—who are they, and where did they come from?" I answered, "Sir, you know." And he said, "These are they who have come out of the great tribulation; they have washed their robes and made them white in the blood of the Lamb. Therefore, they are before the throne of God and serve him day and night in his temple; and he who sits on the throne will shelter them with his presence. Never again will they hunger; never again will they thirst. The sun will not beat down on them, nor any scorching heat. For the Lamb at the center of the throne will be their shepherd; he will lead them to springs of living water. And God will wipe away every tear from their eyes."

Finally, God's patience will come to an end. The great plagues of the Tribulation have started, and they will continue until God says *enough*. The seals seem to be man's wrath against his fellow man. God uses human agents to pour out His wrath against unbelieving men and nations. Angels blow the trumpets. The trumpets seem to be Satan's wrath against man. The vials or bowls are God's direct wrath against man. God says *enough*. The first three and one-half years bring a pseudo-peace. They bring a false peace and security to the world, especially to the nation of Israel. The last half of the seven-year Tribulation Period brings intense wrath and great tribulation.

Now let's look at the four horsemen of the apocalypse. Revelation 6:1-8 reveals,

I watched as the Lamb opened the first of the seven seals. Then I heard one of the four living creatures say in a voice like thunder, "Come!" I looked, and there before me was a white horse! Its rider held a bow, and he was given a crown, and he rode out as a conqueror bent on conquest. When the Lamb opened the second seal, I heard the second living creature say, "Come!" Then another horse came out, a fiery red one. Its rider was given power to take peace from the earth and to make people kill each other. To him was given a large sword. When the Lamb opened the third seal, I heard the third living creature say, "Come!" I looked, and there before me was a black horse! Its rider was holding a pair of scales in his hand. Then I heard what sounded like a voice among the four living creatures, saying, "Two pounds of wheat for a day's wages, and six pounds of barley for a day's wages, and do not damage the oil and the wine!" When the Lamb opened the fourth seal, I heard the voice of the fourth living creature say, "Come!" I looked, and there before me was a pale horse! Its rider was named Death, and Hades was following close behind him. They were given power over a fourth of the earth to kill by sword, famine, and plague, and by the wild beasts of the earth.

Here is the Lamb, opening the seven-sealed scroll book. Here is Jesus Christ, the only one found worthy to open the book. A search was made in Heaven, on earth and even under the earth, and no one was found worthy but Christ. John sees the first horseman riding upon a white horse. At first glance, you might think this is Jesus, like we see in Revelation 19 when Jesus rides on a white horse coming from Heaven. However, in Revelation 6:1-2, this man is not Jesus; it is the Antichrist. The only similarity is the white horse. The Beast will counterfeit the Son's work. Satan during this time period counterfeits the Father's work and the False Prophet will counterfeit the Holy Spirit's work. They comprise the false trinity: the Beast, the False Prophet, and Satan.

The Antichrist holds a bow, but there are no arrows. He goes about to conquer. He is bent on conquest. This is a picture of cold war. He is given a crown. He is given his authority to rule. He would have no authority at all unless it was given to him by God Himself, and that only for a short period of time. Open hostilities have not yet begun. The first seal reveals the Conqueror, the Antichrist.

The red horse is revealed. His rider is given authority to remove peace from the earth. There will be war and open hostilities. Major open conflicts are on the earth. Now is revealed the third horsemen of the apocalypse. Apocalypse means unveiling, disclosure, revelation.

The horsemen have been hidden in the sense of being in the seven-sealed scroll. The seals are broken by Christ, and He allows what has been hidden to be disclosed.

The black horse is revealed with his rider having scales in his hand. There will be a careful rationing of food. This is a dark picture of famine, scarcity, and hunger. There will be extreme inflation. The world's economics today are in a downfall. When will it end? Where will it end? The normal food supply of the world will be greatly decreased. The inflationary rate will skyrocket, and the world will be in great poverty. There will be major scarcity of necessary resources on earth.

If that were not enough, the fourth seal reveals a pale horse, a yellowish green horse. The rider was Death and Hades. Death claims the material part of man, the body. Hades claims the immaterial part of man, the soul. Death and Hades are pictured as riding piggyback. They are given power over the earth to kill by sword (war), by famine (hunger), by plagues (diseases), and by wild beasts on the earth (roaming and killing). There will be widespread death on earth. Here are the first four seal judgments. These seem mild compared to what the trumpet and vial judgments will bring on the earth.

Here is a summary statement about the rest of the seals, the trumpets, and the vials (bowls). The fifth seal is open, and we have the revelation of the cry of the martyrs. The sixth seal reveals cosmic disturbances. The seventh seal is a prelude to the seven trumpets, with silence in Heaven for about half an hour. The seven angels who have the seven trumpets sound them. The first trumpet is blown and earth's vegetation is struck; at the second trumpet, the seas are struck; at the third trumpet, the waters are struck; at the fourth trumpet, the heavens are struck; when the fifth trumpet sounds, the first woe is seen, the locusts from the bottomless pit; the sixth trumpet sounds, and the second woe is seen, the angels from the Euphrates River, and finally the seventh trumpet is blown and loud voices in Heaven speak, and ultimately the seven bowls are poured out.

The first bowl is poured out, and it reveals sores on mankind. The second bowl is poured out on the sea, and water becomes blood with all life dying. The third bowl is poured out on the fresh water supply. The fourth bowl affects the sun as it scorches men. The fifth bowl is judgment on the kingdom/throne/government of the Beast. The sixth bowl dries up the Euphrates River to prepare for the crossing of the armies of the East. The seventh bowl brings widespread destruction: an earthquake in which islands and mountains disappear and hailstones (100 pounds each) fall on mankind.

More is revealed during the last half of the Great Tribulation. Hear now what Revelation 11:10-14 says,

> The inhabitants of the earth will gloat over them and will celebrate by sending each other gifts, because these two prophets had tormented those who live on the earth. But after the three and a half days, the breath of life from God entered them, and they stood on their feet, and terror struck those who saw them. Then they heard a loud voice from heaven saying to them, "Come up here." And they went up to heaven in a cloud, while their enemies looked on. At that very hour there was a severe earthquake and a tenth of the city collapsed. Seven thousand people were killed in the earthquake, and the survivors were terrified and gave glory to the God of heaven. The second woe has passed; the third woe is coming soon.

It is so interesting that this is the only time rejoicing is mentioned during the Tribulation hour on the earth. The two witnesses are killed by the Antichrist and the world rejoices, sending gifts to one another. I call this "Beastmas," for there is no Christmas. There will not be Christendom as we understand it today in the Tribulation, but only "Beastdom." Can't you just picture the scene? The witnesses are killed, and after three and a half days God raised them to life and they were commanded by God to come to Heaven in a cloud while the unbelieving world watches. Can't you just picture the scenario? "This is CNN reporting, 'they just got up!'" At that very hour, there was a great earthquake, and a tenth of Jerusalem falls. Revelation 11:19 says, "Then God's temple in heaven was opened, and within his temple was seen the ark of his covenant. And there came flashes of lightning, rumblings, peals of thunder, an earthquake and a severe hailstorm."

Let's look at the seventh vial judgment in detail. Revelation 16:17-21 reveals the seventh vial or bowl judgment,

> The seventh angel poured out his bowl into the air, and out of the temple came a loud voice from the throne, saying, "It is done!" Then there came flashes of lightning, rumblings, peals of thunder and a severe earthquake. No earthquake like it has ever occurred since mankind has been on earth, so tremendous was the quake. The great city split into three parts, and the cities of the nations collapsed. God remembered Babylon the Great and gave her the cup filled with the wine of the fury of his wrath. Every island fled away and the mountains could not be found. From the sky huge hailstones, each weighing about a hundred pounds, fell on people. And they cursed God on account of the plague of hail, because the plague was so terrible.

Earthquakes are mentioned many times in Revelation, but this earthquake's magnitude has never been equaled before this time. Islands fall into the sea and mountains will be leveled. Huge hailstones about a hundred pounds each fall upon mankind. This is right at the end of the Tribulation hour. The results of the judgments are staggering. Men continue to curse God. It says here men blasphemed God because of the hail. Revelation 9:20-22 says,

> The rest of mankind who were not killed by these plagues still did not repent of the work of their hands; they did not stop worshiping demons, and idols of gold, silver, bronze, stone and wood—idols that cannot see or hear or walk. Nor did they repent of their murders, their magic arts, their sexual immorality or their thefts.

I just want to praise God now for Revelation 3:10, "Since you have kept my command to endure patiently, I will also keep you from the hour of trial that is going to come on the whole world to test the inhabitants of the earth." God will keep us from this seven-year trial that will test those who dwell on the earth. Some repent and turn to God. Many do not. They continue to curse and blaspheme God and His Name. He is the One who has power and authority over these judgments.

We may now ask, "What is the purpose of the Tribulation?" God is still in control, and He is working out His purposes, which are four-fold. First, God will bring an end to what the Word of God calls, the Times of the Gentiles. Jesus speaks loudly and clearly about this in Luke 21:24, "They will fall by the sword and will be taken as prisoners to all the nations. Jerusalem will be trampled on by the Gentiles until the Times of the Gentiles are fulfilled." The Times of the Gentiles is non-Jewish rule over the land promised specifically by covenant to the nation of Israel. This period will end after the Beast is given seven years to conquer and rule. The Times of the Gentiles end when Christ comes back riding on a white horse in Revelation 19.

Second, God will use the Tribulation to prepare the nation of Israel for her Messiah. God will again take up His dealing with Israel as a nation. By means of the Tribulation, God will bring the unbelieving remnant of the nation of Israel to Himself. Jehovah says in Hosea 5:15, "Then I will return to my lair until they have borne their guilt and seek my face—in their misery they will earnestly seek me." Zechariah records in 12:8-10,

> On that day the LORD will shield those who live in Jerusalem, so that the feeblest among them will be like David, and the house of David will be like God, like the angel of the LORD going before them. On that day I will set out to destroy all the nations that attack Jerusalem. And I will pour out on the house of David and the inhabitants of Jerusalem a spirit of grace and supplication. They will look on me, the one they have pierced, and they will mourn for him as one mourns for an only child, and grieve bitterly for him as one grieves for a firstborn son.

Revelation 1:7 concurs, "Look, he is coming with the clouds, and every eye will see him, even those who pierced him and all peoples on earth will mourn because of him. So shall it be! Amen." The prophet Zechariah also says in 13:1, "On that day a fountain will be opened to the house of David and the inhabitants of Jerusalem, to cleanse them from sin and impurity." Israel will turn to Jehovah God, our Lord Jesus Christ, Her Messiah and our Messiah.

Third, God will pour out His judgment on unbelieving men and nations. From the fall of Jerusalem under King Nebuchadnezzar to the Second Coming of Jesus Christ, we have been living in the Times of the Gentiles (Luke 21:24). God will judge the Gentile nations of the world on how they treated His elect and chosen people, the children of Abraham, the nation of Israel.

Fourth, God will judge apostate Christendom (what I call, "Beastdom"). The Tribulation will mark a climactic judgment upon apostate Christendom ("Beastdom"). It is the harlot of Revelation 17:16-17. It will be a commercial, economic, political, and religious system (Revelation 17-18).

We do not know the exact time and date of the Tribulation. It is in the future. It will begin with one specific event, the making of the peace pact by the man of sin with the nation of Israel (Daniel 9:27). It is the period of Daniel's seventieth week (Daniel 9:24-27). The Tribulation will begin with the making of the covenant. It will proceed for seven years. It will conclude when Christ comes and judges the Beast and the False Prophet at the Battle of Armageddon (Revelation 16:16).

Before we go on to chapter five, "The Great Triumph," let me share with you a summary of the Book of Revelation, all twenty-two chapters. The Great Tribulation covers chapters 6-18, the bulk of the Book of Revelation.

Here is the summary of each chapter of the Book of Revelation:

Chapter:

1: Greeting to the seven churches of Asia Minor and the Vision of the Son of Man.

2: *Ephesus,* the loveless church; *Smyrna,* the persecuted church; *Pergamos,* the compromising church, and *Thyatira,* the corrupt church.

3: *Sardis,* the dead church; *Philadelphia,* the faithful church, and *Laodicea,* the lukewarm church.

4: "Come up here," spoken to John by Jesus. John was at once in the Spirit in the throne room of Heaven with the 24 elders and 4 living creatures. The Apostle John here is the picture of the Rapture, where it would occur naturally in the Book of Revelation. Perhaps this is the loud command (shout) of 1 Thessalonians 4:16!

5: The Lamb takes the scroll out of the Father's hand and praise to the Lamb who is worthy breaks out.

6: The first seal, the Conqueror; the second seal, conflict on Earth; the third seal, scarcity on earth; the fourth seal, widespread death on Earth; the fifth seal, the cry of the martyrs, and the sixth seal, cosmic disturbances.

7: The 144,000 sealed of Israel and a great multitude saved from the Great Tribulation.

8: The seventh seal, prelude to the seven trumpets with silence in Heaven for about half an hour; the first trumpet, vegetation struck; the second trumpet, the seas struck; the third trumpet, the waters struck, and the fourth trumpet, the heavens struck.

9: The fifth trumpet, first woe, the locusts from the bottomless pit; the sixth trumpet, the second woe, the angels from the Euphrates River.

10: The Mighty Angel (King Jesus) and the little book; John eats the book.

11: The two mighty witnesses' (the two lampstands and olive trees standing before the Lord of the earth) testimony for three and one-half years, and then they are killed, raised, and translated to Heaven; the seventh trumpet, the Kingdom is proclaimed and praise from the twenty-four elders starts in Heaven.

12: War is revealed on earth, in Heaven, and then back on earth; two wonders presented: the woman is Israel and the dragon is Satan; Michael and His angels fight with the dragon and his army; the dragon and his army are cast out of Heaven for good, and now Satan vehemently attacks God's people, especially the woman (Israel).

13: The Beast rises out of the sea (the masses of people, the Gentiles); his Kingdom is revealed composing the Western confederation of nations—the revived Roman Empire; the Beast is full of blasphemy and war extends to all people except those whose names are in the Book of Life; the False Prophet rises from the earth (the Land), and he promotes worship of the first Beast and performs many miracles.

14: The 144,000 are seen again with the Lamb in Heaven; next, an angel appears announcing the everlasting gospel to all the world; Babylon's doom is predicted by another angel (the fall of Babylon is described in detail in chapters 17 and 18); a third angel announces judgment on all who worship the Beast, and the earth is harvested while some are taken into the kingdom blessing (Millennium) and others go into judgment (Hades).

15: The prelude to the last judgments of the Tribulation hour; seven golden vials contain the wrath of God.

16: The first bowl poured out reveals sores on mankind; the second bowl is poured out on the sea and water becomes blood (with all marine life dying); the third bowl is poured out on the fresh water supply; the fourth bowl affects the sun to scorch men; the fifth bowl is judgment on the kingdom/throne/government of the Beast; the sixth bowl poured out dries up the Euphrates River to prepare the crossing of the armies of the East, and the seventh bowl brings widespread destruction: a severe earthquake where islands and mountains disappear, and hailstones (100 pounds each) fall on mankind.

17: Babylon is presented as a city and a system, religious and political; she is destroyed by the Beast who alone commands worship.

18: Babylon is presented commercially (economically) as demonic, unfaithful, and intoxicating; she is judged and kings and merchants lament her demise.

19: The marriage of the Lamb is seen in Heaven as the Bride of Christ is married to Him; Christ then comes back riding on a white horse and the hosts of Heaven (saints and angels) return with Him and He will be Conqueror and Victor at the Battle of Armageddon (Revelation 16:16).

20: The Millennium is pictured as one thousand years; Satan is bound in the abyss and released for a short season after the Millennium; Satan is cast into Gehenna where he will be tormented forever, and the Great White Throne judgment is set where the lost of all ages are judged and then cast into the lake of fire, the second death.

21: This chapter begins the eternal state; the New Jerusalem descends from Heaven and God makes all things new; the city is described as glorious with twelve gates (pearls) and twelve foundations (precious stones); the wall is adorned with jasper and the city is pure gold; the foundation is adorned with many precious stones, and *Paradise is realized!*

22: Words of comfort are given; three times Jesus says, "I come quickly;" God is worthy of worship; rewards are given; the redeemed are blessed; and all are warned (our generation today) not to add to or subtract from the words of prophecy of the Book of Revelation, and the customary benediction is "The grace of the Lord Jesus be with God's people. Amen" (Revelation 22:21).

Note: A great resource on the subject matter of this chapter is the work by Jack Van Impe, *Revelation Revealed*.

FIVE

The Great Triumph

A day of the LORD is coming, Jerusalem, when your possessions will be plundered and divided up within your
very walls. I will gather all the nations to Jerusalem to
fight against it; the city will be captured, the houses ran-
sacked, and the women raped. Half of the city will go into
exile, but the rest of the people will not be taken from
the city. Then the LORD will go out and fight against those
nations, as he fights on a day of battle. On that day his feet
will stand on the Mount of Olives, east of Jerusalem, and
the Mount of Olives will be split in two from east to west,
forming a great valley, with half of the mountain moving
north and half moving south. You will flee by my mountain
valley, for it will extend to Azel. You will flee as you fled
from the earthquake in the days of Uzziah king of Judah.
Then the LORD my God will come, and all the holy ones
with him. (Zechariah 14:1-5)

These verses give us a picture of what it will be like when Jesus
Christ is revealed from Heaven and comes back at the end of
the Tribulation hour. Today, we are living in the inter-advent
age. It is the period of time between the first advent of Jesus Christ
and His second advent. The birth of Christ in Bethlehem was His

82

first coming. He has promised He is coming to the earth again. He lived on the earth for thirty-three years the first time. At His second coming, He will dwell on the earth for one thousand years. We call that period of time the Millennium. We will cover the Millennium in the next chapter. The second coming of Jesus Christ is in two phases. The first phase is what we have already covered. It is the Rapture. He comes for His Bride, the Church. He comes for us. He comes in the air. The second phase of the second coming of Jesus Christ is the Revelation. We come back with Him. At the first phase His feet will not touch the earth, but at the second phase His feet will touch the earth again. Praise to our Lord and Savior Jesus Christ! He will come in power and glory to reign on the earth. The definition of the great triumph is the return of Christ to the Earth after the Tribulation to put down all His enemies and to establish His Messianic Kingdom. This is the great triumph of Jesus Christ. He is coming back as King of kings and Lord of lords. He will put down all His enemies and He will establish His Messianic reign over this world for one thousand years.

There are many pertinent things to know about the great triumph. First, it will be personal. Matthew 24:27-30 says,

> For as lightning that comes from the east is visible even in the west, so will be the coming of the Son of Man. Wherever there is a carcass, there the vultures will gather. Immediately after the distress of those days the sun will be darkened, and the moon will not give its light; the stars will fall from the sky, and the heavenly bodies will be shaken. Then will appear the sign of the Son of Man in heaven. And then all the peoples of the earth will mourn when they see the Son of Man coming on the clouds of heaven, with power and great glory.

Jesus Christ is coming back Himself; no one else in His place, not even an angel, not even Michael or Gabriel. Jesus will come. Matthew 24 in context is the Tribulation hour. Jesus used the title Son of Man for Himself more than any other title. He has completely identified with mankind. He became one of us at His incarnation.

John said in John 1:14, "The Word became flesh and made his dwelling among us. We have seen his glory, the glory of the one and only Son, who came from the Father, full of grace and truth."

The Son of God became man. He became the Son of Man. He has two natures, both God and man. He is the Theanthropic Person. This means that Jesus Christ is the God Man, one person with two natures. Jesus said the Son of Man is coming with power and great glory. He even told His enemies He would personally be coming back. In Mark 14:61-62 we read, "But Jesus remained silent and gave no answer. Again the high priest asked him, 'Are you the Messiah, the Son of the Blessed One?' 'I am,' said Jesus 'And you will see the Son of Man sitting at the right hand of the Mighty One and coming on the clouds of heaven.'" Jesus is coming back, but as recorded in Mark 14, Jesus was on trial before Caiaphas. He was the actual High Priest at the time, but behind him stood his father-in-law, Annas, who wielded the ultimate authority and power of the priesthood. Caiaphas was simply a figurehead. The high priest Caiaphas questioned Jesus to ascertain if He were the Christ, the Son of God. Jesus answered, "I am," and spoke of His Revelation from Heaven. Jesus was saying that He is Jehovah God. John's Gospel records seven great *I Ams* of Christ. It will be a personal return after the Tribulation hour (from the context of Mark 14).

Second, His coming will be bodily. Zechariah was a minor prophet. He wrote about 500 years before Jesus Christ. He wrote about the return of Christ, the Revelation of Jesus Christ. In Zechariah 14 we read again, "A day of the LORD is coming, Jerusalem, when your possessions will be plundered and divided up within your very walls" (Zechariah 14:1). We see here the Day of the LORD. It is a time of judgment on the earth. It is the time of Jacob's Trouble. The Church is gone; we have been evacuated. This is a day of doom, gloom, distress, vengeance, cloud, judgment, and punishment. The Day of Christ is the Day of the Rapture. The Day of the LORD is the Day of the Revelation. God will gather all the nations against Jerusalem to fight against it. God is the One who engineers it. God is Sovereign and He reigns yesterday, today, and forever. The Gentiles will say, "We have Jerusalem back from the Jews once more." So much suffering will happen, such as rape, exile, and plunder. So many atrocities and social injustices will take place. Revelation appropriately sums up mankind's treatment of his fellow man in several passages. Revelation 9:21 says, "Nor did they repent of their murders, their magic arts, their sexual immorality or their thefts." Revelation 16:9-11 says,

> They were seared by the intense heat and they cursed the name of God, who had control over these plagues, but they refused to repent and glorify him. The fifth angel poured out his bowl on the throne of the beast, and its kingdom was plunged into darkness. People gnawed their tongues in agony and cursed the God of heaven because of their pains and their sores, but they refused to repent of what they had done.

The Lord will fight against the nations coming against Israel for war. So many times in the Old Testament Jehovah God was Israel's Commander-in-Chief. He went before them into battle. One example was when Moses led God's chosen people out of Egypt after 430 years in bondage. Moses and the children of Israel were trapped in the desert, Pharaoh and his armies were behind them, and the Red Sea in front. Moses spoke these words to Israel, "The LORD will fight for you; you need only to be still" (Exodus 14:14). The day of battle simply means that God anywhere and anytime will supernaturally deliver His people. There is going to be another day of battle, the time when the nations are gathered in Jerusalem at the Revelation of Jesus Christ, the great triumph. His second coming to the earth will put down all His enemies and establish His Messianic Kingdom.

What a glorious day! The Gentiles, following the Beast and the False Prophet, will think they have won the day in Jerusalem. When all hope seems lost and when the world seems so wicked that it can endure no more, Christ comes. Jesus paralleled it with the account of Noah. In Noah's day the earth was full of evil,

> Now the earth was corrupt in God's sight and was full of violence. God saw how corrupt the earth had become, for all the people on earth had corrupted their ways. So

85

> God said to Noah,"I am going to put an end to all people, for the earth is filled with violence because of them. I am surely going to destroy both them and the earth." (Genesis 6:11-13)

Jesus spoke this way about this time in Luke 17:26-27: "Just as it was in the days of Noah, so also will it be in the days of the Son of Man. People were eating, drinking, marrying and being given in marriage up to the day Noah entered the ark. Then the flood came and destroyed them all." The prophecy of Zechariah 14:1-4 speaks of the Lord's feet standing on the Mount of Olives on that day of battle. I stood on the Mount of Olives in the year 2000. It was a life-changing event for my teenage son and me to travel to the Holy Land. From the Mount of Olives looking toward the west, the Old City of Jerusalem and the New City of Jerusalem can be seen. The Eastern Gate can also be seen. It is from the same Mount of Olives that our Lord Jesus Christ ascended to Heaven and will descend from Heaven at the end of the Tribulation hour at the great triumph. His feet will indeed stand on that same Mount He stood on almost two thousand years ago and where I stood over a decade ago.

What a glorious day! Jesus is coming back to this earth to reign. His coming will be bodily. In the Old Testament Jehovah did not have feet (unless there was a revelation of Jehovah when He revealed Himself in a Theophany or Christophany). A Theophany is a visible and physical (in the flesh) manifestation of God in the Old Testament. Some examples of Theophanies are found in Genesis 17:1; 18:1; Exodus 6:2-3; 24:9-11; and Numbers 12:6-8. I believe all physical appearances of God in the Old Testament were the pre-incarnate Christ, because no one has ever seen the Father (John 6:46). Jehovah came to earth born in human flesh. The Word became flesh. The Word dwelt among us. Jehovah God became man in His incarnation. Jesus ascended into Heaven bodily, and He will descend bodily at the end of the Great Tribulation. At that time His feet will touch the earth again. He is coming back in His same resurrected, ascended, glorified body.

When this event happens, the Mount of Olives will be split from east to west. A great valley will be formed. The Mount will move north and south. Great geographical and topographical changes will take place at the great triumph. These changes continue with many more happening when Jesus sets up His Kingdom on the earth for one thousand years, called the Millennium. We will look at the great ten centuries in the next chapter. The curse on creation will be lifted during this time and the earth will experience a new birth.

Zechariah 14:5 speaks of this new valley formed by Jesus Christ, and it is the pathway for His people to flee on when He returns. It reads, "You will flee by my mountain valley, for it will extend to Azel. You will flee as you fled from the earthquake in the days of Uzziah king of Judah. Then the LORD my God will come, and all the holy ones with him." Jesus will prepare the way. He is the Way, the Truth, and the Life (John 14:6). God's people will be under great persecution and assault by the nations of the world. Jerusalem will be under siege and will be taken. Half the population will go into captivity, but God allows a remnant of His people to remain in Jerusalem. This remnant will flee like the Israelites fled when the earthquake in the days of King Uzziah of Judah shook the land. People still in Jerusalem at the end of the Great Tribulation can flee through that passageway, through the valley Jesus forms on that day. He is the Way. His people are going to be delivered. Amos the minor prophet speaks of the earthquake in Amos 1:1, "The words of Amos, one of the shepherds of Tekoa—the vision he saw concerning Israel two years before the earthquake, when Uzziah was king of Judah and Jeroboam son of Jehoash was king of Israel." Amos began his prophecy two years before the earthquake in Uzziah's reign over Judah. Excavators at Hazor (in present day Israel) found evidence of an earthquake, which they date to about 760 B.C. The Lord has used earthquakes in history, past and present, and will use them mightily during the Tribulation period of seven years on the earth. Zechariah 14:5 also reveals that "the LORD my God will come, and all the holy ones with Him." This is the time of the great triumph when we come back with our Lord Jesus Christ as seen in Revelation, chapter 19, especially verse 14: "The armies of heaven were following him, riding on white horses and dressed in fine linen, white and clean." So, we have seen that at the time of Christ's Second Advent, God will provide the spiritual and physical deliverance for His people when it seems all hope is gone. The Lord our God will come! Five hundred years before Jesus Christ, Zechariah spoke of the Lord my God. Zechariah believed in the Lord's coming. He is coming to rule the world in righteousness and peace.

Third, Jesus is coming back visibly. Revelation 1:7 says, "Look, he is coming with the clouds, and every eye will see him, even those who pierced him and all peoples on earth will mourn because of him. So shall it be! Amen." Jesus, during His public ministry on earth at His first advent, said several times He would be coming with clouds. Revelation 1:7 reveals that every eye will see Him, all peoples on earth, even the Jews who pierced Him. This is *not* the Rapture. The Rapture is a private viewing only for the redeemed of this age, the Church Age, the Age of Grace. Only dead and living saints from the inception of the Church, until His appearing in the clouds, called the Rapture, will see Him at this time. The world will *not* see Him. However, at the Revelation of Jesus Christ at the end of the Tribulation period, all eyes will see Him. Some will look at Him for deliverance from the Antichrist and his False Prophet. Some will mourn, for He is coming in vengeance and judgment. Christ will be visible for every eye to see. Where do you stand with Jesus Christ? When every eye sees Him on this day, how will that happen? Could it be by satellite, Internet, television, or even social media? Some say, He will stay in the air while the earth rotates for twenty-four hours, so the world will see Him that way. Perhaps the best way to view it is that all will see Him supernaturally. All will see His brightness and His glory. However God accomplishes this, it will take place and Christ's coming will be visible for all to see.

Fourth, Jesus' coming will be Pre-millennial. Revelation, chapter 19, is the most detailed place in the Scriptures that teaches the second coming of Christ. There are many other passages teaching His Revelation at the Second Advent. Let's look at Revelation, chapter 19. It reads, beginning in verse eleven,

I saw heaven standing open and there before me was a white horse, whose rider is called Faithful and True. With justice he judges and wages war. His eyes are like blazing fire, and on his head are many crowns. He has a name written on him that no one knows but he himself. He is dressed in a robe dipped in blood, and his name is the Word of God. The armies of heaven were following him, riding on white horses and dressed in fine linen, white and clean. Coming out of his mouth is a sharp sword with which to strike down the nations. He will rule them with an iron scepter. He treads the winepress of the fury of the wrath of God Almighty. On his robe and on his thigh he has this name written: KING OF KINGS AND LORD OF LORDS. And I saw an angel standing in the sun, who cried in a loud voice to all the birds flying in midair, "Come, gather together for the great supper of God, so that you may eat the flesh of kings, generals, and the mighty, of horses and their riders, and the flesh of all people, free and slave, great and small." Then I saw the beast and the kings of the earth and their armies gathered together to wage war against the rider on the horse and his army. But the beast was captured, and with it the false prophet who had performed the signs on its behalf. With these signs he had deluded those who had received the mark of the beast and worshiped its image. The two of them were thrown alive into the fiery lake of burning sulfur. The rest were killed with the sword coming out of the mouth of the rider on the horse, and all the birds gorged themselves on their flesh. (Revelation 19:11-21)

All this reveals a different scenario from the Rapture. The Great Triumph or Revelation of Christ reveals Jesus coming back on a white horse, Faithful and True. At this coming, He judges and wages war in righteousness. His whole appearance, demeanor, and action are totally different from what will take place at the Rapture. Premillennial teaching is that Jesus Christ will come back before the establishment of the one thousand-year reign. He will come back at the end of the Tribulation period, end the Battle of Armageddon, judge the sheep and goats, establish His Kingdom, and then reign over the earth for one thousand years. This is literal. It should be taken as literal. There is no allegory here, no spiritual application that would negate the literal rule of Jesus Christ on the Throne of David, the Son of David, on the throne in Jerusalem. We can't spiritualize the Scripture and say that Jesus is reigning now on David's throne, the Church is "Spiritual Israel," and all the covenant blessings promised to Israel have been transferred to the Church with no literal fulfillment. The Amillennial approach just described doesn't make sense. If the literal sense makes good sense, look for no other sense. This is a good rule of thumb in the interpretation of God's Word. Revelation 19 teaches the Revelation of Christ riding on a white horse as being Pre-millennial.

Fifth, Christ's coming will be Post-tribulational when His Revelation takes place. Christ is coming after the Tribulation period. The first phase of Christ's coming is the Rapture, before the Tribulation. Jesus will save His Church from wrath, Hell, and the great testing that will try everyone living on the earth during the Tribulation period (Matthew 24:21-31).

The carcass is Israel, and the vultures are the nations of the world (Matthew 24:28). The nations will be like vultures to consume Israel. Even today in our generation, several nations would like to consume Israel, push her into the Mediterranean Sea, or see a bright flash of light over her (nuclear destruction). Israel is termed the *little Satan*. America is termed the *big Satan*. The birds of prey surround Jerusalem. Remember what Zechariah wrote in chapter 14, verses one and two,

> A day of the LORD is coming, Jerusalem, when your possessions will be plundered and divided up within your very walls. I will gather all the nations to Jerusalem to fight against it; the city will be captured, the houses ransacked, and the women raped. Half of the city will go into exile, but the rest of the people will not be taken from the city.

Israel must go through this time of purging and cleansing, but Jesus confirms for us for us that Israel will be delivered (Matthew 24:29-30). We have already seen in Revelation 1:7 concerning His appearing that the nations will mourn, Israel will look on Him whom they have pierced, and every eye will see Jesus at the end of the Great Tribulation.

Finally, under pertinent things to know about the Revelation of Christ, His coming will be glorious. He comes with power and great glory. Matthew 25:31 says, "When the Son of Man comes in his glory, and all the angels with him, he will sit on his glorious throne." Jesus will sit upon the throne of His glory in Jerusalem, finally a "City of Peace," and peace will last for one thousand years. At the end of the Millennium, the "City of Peace," the camp of the saints and the beloved city (Jerusalem) will be besieged by those who have been deceived by Satan (Revelation 20:7-10). When Jesus comes at His Revelation, war will cease, and the Kingdom of our Lord and Christ will be one of righteousness and peace. "The seventh angel sounded his trumpet, and there were loud voices in heaven, which said: 'The kingdom of the world has become the kingdom of our Lord and of his Messiah, and he will reign for ever and ever'" (Revelation 11:15).

This will be a good time to look at the distinguishing marks of the Rapture and Revelation, the two phases of the Second Advent of Jesus Christ. First, the time when each will take place. The Rapture is before the Tribulation, and the Revelation is after the Tribulation. Revelation 1:19 says, "'Write, therefore, what you have seen, what is now and what will take place later.'" Jesus is speaking to John the Apostle. This verse forms a natural outline for the Book of Revelation. John was told to write *the things he had seen;* it refers to chapter one of the book. Write *the things happening now* refers to chapters two and three of the book. Then John was told to write about the *things that would take place later* (chapters four through twenty-two of the Book of Revelation). In Revelation 4:1 the Apostle John was commanded by God to come to Heaven and be shown the things that must take place after this. John immediately was in the Spirit, in Heaven. Here, John is a type of what will take place for the Church of Jesus Christ at the Rapture. When the command is issued we will be caught up to Heaven to be with the Bridegroom, our Lord Jesus Christ (1 Thessalonians 4). At this point in the Book of Revelation, the Rapture will take place. Revelation 19 speaks of a different appearing of Christ. John, again, sees Heaven opened.

Revelation 19:11 says, "I saw heaven standing open and there before me was a white horse, whose rider is called Faithful and True. With justice he judges and wages war."

Second, the place for each event is different. For the Rapture, it is in the air. First Thessalonians 4:17 says, "After that, we who are still alive and are left will be caught up together with them in the clouds to meet the Lord in the air. And so we will be with the Lord forever." Jesus takes us back to Heaven with Him where we will stand before the Judgment Seat (*Bema*) of Christ. The Revelation of Christ teaches that Jesus' feet will touch the earth, specifically, the Mount of Olives (Zechariah 14:3-5). Jesus' feet will touch terra firma again to reign for one thousand years.

Third, who are the subjects at the Rapture and Revelation? At the Rapture the subjects are the members of Christ's Body, the Church. Only believers of the Church Age will see Him at the Rapture. At the Revelation, though, all people will see Him. In the Old Testament, the Rapture was a mystery and the Revelation was a promise in prophecy. A mystery is a truth unknown and unknowable apart from God's Divine Revelation. The Rapture is seen only in type in the Old Testament. Enoch and Elijah are types of the Rapture. What was the mystery? The mystery revealed in the New Testament is that a large group of people would not die when Jesus Christ comes back in the air. This is the Rapture generation. I am Rapture ready! A large group of people will be changed without experiencing death and resurrection. At the Rapture, all must be changed in a flash, in the twinkling of an eye as seen in 1 Corinthians 15. I would love to be part of the Rapture in the "alive in Christ" category, but the dead in Christ will rise first. This truth from God was revealed to the Apostle Paul as He wrote the book of 1 Thessalonians. Please get this truth. A large group of people will not die and will ascend into Heaven with Christ. We also, will, without dying or being resurrected, ascend with the dead in Christ. Maranatha!

The Revelation of Christ's coming to set up His Kingdom is seen over and over again in holy writ. One place is in Isaiah 24:23, "The moon will be dismayed, the sun ashamed; for the Lord Almighty will reign on Mount Zion and in Jerusalem, and before its elders—with great glory." The Second Coming of Jesus Christ at the Revelation is prophesied over and over again in the Old Testament. The Lord is coming, and His Coming is promised over and over again. His feet will touch the Mount of Olives. He will stand on the earth. However things are different at the Rapture. Isaiah wrote Isaiah 24:23 seven hundred years before Christ, whose first coming is well documented in the Gospels and other New Testament books. Was Isaiah 24:23 fulfilled at His first advent? No. He did not come to reign, although after feeding the four thousand and the five thousand, the crowds wanted to make Him King. He refused to bypass God's will at His first coming. God's will for Jesus was to do the works of the Father and to complete His work. Hear Jesus speak, "I have testimony weightier than that of John. For the works that the Father has given me to finish—the very works that I am doing—testify that the Father has sent me" (John 5:36). He came to go to the cross to die for all the sins of all mankind. God's work is seen so lovingly in John 3:16-17, "For God so loved the world that he gave his one and only Son, that whoever believes in him shall not perish but have eternal life. For God did not send his Son into the world to condemn the world, but to save the world through him."

Another distinguishing mark between the Rapture and the Revelation is the visibility. The Rapture is only for the Church. The visibility for the Revelation is for the whole world—all the world at the time of Christ's coming back to reign. It will be a public viewing, very public. Are you ready to meet Christ at His Coming? Both are also different in purpose. At the Rapture, Jesus Christ is coming back for us. At the Revelation we are coming back with Him.

The final mark is the concept of one left and one taken. At the Rapture, the believer is taken, and the unbeliever is left. At the Revelation, the unbeliever is taken, and the believer is left. At the Rapture, when Jesus comes for His own people, the unbeliever is left, and he has no say so in the matter. At the Revelation, the unbeliever is taken, and he has no say in the matter. He is taken to stand in judgment. It will be the judgment of the sheep and the goats. The believer remains on the earth to go into the Millennial Kingdom with Jesus Christ. Those who make it through the Tribulation will go into the Millennium in their natural bodies and children will be born to them during the Millennium. Even death will take place during the one thousand years. There are many truths about the Millennium. We will see these in the next chapter.

Hear Jesus speak in Matthew 24:36-46,

> But about that day or hour no one knows, not even the angels in heaven, nor the Son, but only the Father. As it was in the days of Noah, so it will be at the coming of the Son of Man. For in the days before the flood, people were eating and drinking, marrying and giving in marriage, up to the day Noah entered the ark; and they knew nothing about what would happen until the flood came and took them all away. That is how it will be at the coming of the Son of Man. Two men will be in the field; one will be taken and the other left. Two women will be grinding with a hand mill; one will be taken and the other left. Therefore keep watch, because you do not know on what day your Lord will come. But understand this: If the owner of the house had known at what time of night the thief was coming, he would have kept watch and would not have let his house be broken into. So you also must be ready, because the Son of Man will come at an hour when you do not expect him. Who then is the faithful and wise servant, whom the master has put in charge of the servants in his household to give them their food at the proper time? It will be good for that servant whose master finds him doing so when he returns.

Look at the context of Matthew 24 and 25. The Great Tribulation is being described. At this time, we see normal daily activities taking place. Noah, the "preacher of righteousness," preached to his generation for one hundred and twenty years. His name means comfort. He was only able to comfort the eight who entered the ark before God shut the door. Everyone outside was not comforted; they met a horrible death. The people did not believe the message. I believe his message; more importantly, I believe Christ's message. I am to watch. I do not know when my Lord is coming.

There are no signs for the Rapture. There will be a multitude of signs for the Revelation. Many will be saved during the Tribulation after the Rapture. Jesus speaks concerning the midpoint of this time to His own people. He warns of the abomination of desolation. Daniel spoke of the abomination of desolation. When these people see it standing in the Temple in the holy place, they will flee from Judea and into the mountains. Jesus gave many other commands in verses 15-20 of Matthew 24. After that, He says in verse 21, "For then there will be great distress, unequaled from the beginning of the world until now—and never to be equaled again." Daniel also speaks of this time. He says in Daniel 12:1, "At that time Michael, the great prince who protects your people, will arise. There will be a time of distress such as has not happened from the beginning of nations until then. But at that time your people—everyone whose name is found written in the book—will be delivered."

Both Old and New Testaments predict signs of the end times pointing to the Revelation of Jesus Christ and the "great distress" before His Revelation (Revelation 19). I believe many of these signs are already in their fulfillment mode. See Matthew 24, Mark 13, and Luke 21. I believe Israel becoming a nation on May 14, 1948, is one of the greatest signs fulfilled in our generation. "Who has ever heard of such things? Who has ever seen things like this? Can a country be born in a day or a nation be brought forth in a moment? Yet no sooner is Zion in labor than she gives birth to her children" (Isaiah 66:8). Israel was reborn as a nation in one day. Israel had been brought back to life in fulfillment of Ezekiel, chapters 36 and 37.

Consider the following partial list of signs from the Old and New Testaments: the alignment of nations in a Western Confederation; wars and rumors of wars; revolutions; lawlessness; famines; earthquakes in different places; pestilences; iniquity abounding; the knowledge explosion; world-wide travel; Israel dwelling in safety, and many more. Check out Joel Rosenberg's sites (websites, books, blogs, etc.) for a look at "Gog and Magog" in Ezekiel 38 and 39. While Israel is dwelling securely (not necessarily meaning at peace), there will be an alignment of nations who will come against Israel (Russia, Iran, and many others). The prophecies are definitely part of the birth pains happening today. We cannot say for sure when the war of Gog and Magog will happen. I believe it could happen soon, even in our lifetime. The current events and trends in the Middle East seem to show us that these events could be much closer to fulfillment than the world realizes. The events today parallel the prophecies of Ezekiel. The prophecies of chapters 36 and 37 have literally come to pass. A nation was reborn after being dispersed from their land for almost 2,000 years. God made this statement concerning Israel, "After many days you will be called to arms. In future years you will invade a land that has recovered from war, whose people were gathered from many nations to the mountains of Israel, which had long been desolate. They had been brought out from the nations, and now all of them live in safety" (Ezekiel 38:8).

Some may say, "There have always been wars, famines, pestilences, and earthquakes; what makes these signs different from what has already been?" That is a very good question. God has provided the answer; a woman in labor giving birth to a child. Did you just read that? Yes, you did. "While people are saying, 'Peace and safety,' destruction will come on them suddenly, as labor pains on a pregnant woman, and they will not escape" (1 Thessalonians 5:3). Look at this verse in the greater context of 1 Thessalonians 5:1-11 that speaks of the Day of Lord:

> Now, brothers and sisters, about times and dates we do not need to write to you, for you know very well that the day of the Lord will come like a thief in the night. While people are saying, "Peace and safety," destruction will come on them suddenly, as labor pains on a pregnant woman, and they will not escape. But you, brothers and sisters, are not in darkness so that this day should surprise you like a thief. You are all children of the light and children of the day. We do not belong to the night or to the darkness. So then, let us not be like others, who are asleep, but let us be awake and sober. For those who sleep, sleep at night, and those who get drunk, get drunk at night. But since we belong to the day, let us be sober, putting on faith and love as a breastplate, and the hope of salvation as a helmet. For God did not appoint us to suffer wrath but to receive

> salvation through our Lord Jesus Christ. He died for us so
> that, whether we are awake or asleep, we may live together
> with him. Therefore encourage one another and build each
> other up, just as in fact you are doing.

In context of 1 Thessalonians, Paul speaks about "labor pains on a pregnant woman." He was not the only one to speak that way.

> Jesus left the temple and was walking away when his dis-
> ciples came up to him to call his attention to its buildings.
> "Do you see all these things?" he asked. "Truly I tell you,
> not one stone here will be left on another; every one will
> be thrown down." As Jesus was sitting on the Mount of
> Olives, the disciples came to him privately. "Tell us," they
> said, "when will this happen, and what will be the sign of
> your coming and of the end of the age?" Jesus answered:
> "Watch out that no one deceives you. For many will come
> in my name, claiming, "I am the Messiah," and will deceive
> many. You will hear of wars and rumors of wars, but see
> to it that you are not alarmed. Such things must happen,
> but the end is still to come. Nation will rise against nation,
> and kingdom against kingdom. There will be famines and
> earthquakes in various places. All these are the beginning
> of birth pains." (Matthew 24:1-8)

Jesus spoke of signs as birth pains. They will have a beginning and an end.

What am I trying to say? A woman who is pregnant and starts labor begins with mild pains that are far apart. The labor continues until the pains are very great and close together. After four children, I really know what that means; I mean, my wife really knows! The point is that when the signs begin to all take place at one time with intensity and rapidity, then, understand that the end of the age is near. What is the sign of the Revelation of Jesus Christ, The Great Triumph (Revelation 19) and the end of the age? The world will be engulfed in distress and trouble neither seen before nor will ever be seen again. Just look at current events in our world. We see hunger, poverty, pestilences, wars (many civil wars, Libya, Egypt, Syria, etc.), rumors of wars (especially Iran with Israel and Russia with Ukraine), distress among nations, and world markets on the borderline of collapse. We see the beginning of America and Great Britain's isolation from the "hot spots" in the world. We see false christs as "nation will rise against nation, and kingdom against kingdom" (Matthew 24:7). Many other disasters are on the horizon.

Our world today is filled with many dangers. Christians are being persecuted in Asia (China), Africa, especially Egypt, and the Middle East, especially Syria and Pakistan. Chemical weapons are being used. The threat of nuclear war is in reach of many evil nations. Some already have the capability to use weapons from their nuclear arsenal. Terrorism is on the rise and will continue. The Antichrist will be the greatest terrorist the world has ever seen. When you combine all the above with massive storms world-wide, floods, forest fires, economies collapsing, and earthquakes all over the world, you can't help but to say that the world is not getting better; evil is increasing. God is continually warning us. We are to act on His wisdom. Are you ready for the Rapture? Get ready by trusting in Jesus Christ and living for Him. Serve Him with honor, integrity, and truth. *Be Rapture ready!*

The intensity and rapidity will increase, and give birth to a time of trouble unequaled before or ever will be again on the earth (Daniel 12:1; Matthew 24:21). Let's look at one example—earthquakes. Earthquakes have been around a long time. Calvary shook. When Jesus died on the Cross, there was an earthquake.

At that moment the curtain of the temple was torn in two from top to bottom. The earth shook, the rocks split and the tombs broke open. The bodies of many holy people who had died were raised to life. They came out of the tombs after Jesus' resurrection and went into the holy city and appeared to many people. When the centurion and those with him who were guarding Jesus saw the earthquake and all that had happened, they were terrified, and exclaimed, "Surely he was the Son of God!" (Matthew 27:51-54)

On the day of Christ's resurrection, there was an earthquake (Matthew 28:2). It is described as violent. Another violent earthquake took place in Philippi when Paul and Silas were in prison (Acts 16:26).

Even today, there are multitudes of earthquakes all around our world. All the earthquakes the world has experienced so far cannot compare to the one described in the Book of Revelation. Here is the description found in Revelation 16:16-21:

> Then they gathered the kings together to the place that in Hebrew is called Armageddon. The seventh angel poured out his bowl into the air, and out of the temple came a loud voice from the throne, saying, "It is done!" Then there came flashes of lightning, rumblings, peals of thunder and a severe earthquake. No earthquake like it has ever occurred since mankind has been on earth, so tremendous was the quake. The great city split into three parts, and the cities of the nations collapsed. God remembered Babylon the Great and gave her the cup filled with the wine of the fury of his wrath. Every island fled away and the mountains could not be found. From the sky huge hailstones, each weighing about a hundred pounds, fell on people. And they cursed God on account of the plague of hail, because the plague was so terrible.

I am a literalist. I believe what God's Word says about this earthquake. It occurs at the end of the Great Tribulation. There has never been one like it in history. As you read through the Book of Revelation, you will find other examples of earthquakes (Revelation 6:12; 8:5; 11:13; 11:19). However, the earthquake in chapter 16 tops them all: cities collapsing within all nations, islands and mountains disappearing, hailstones weighing one hundred pounds falling on people. You talk about intensity and rapidity of judgment and signs being fulfilled; we have it all here. It seems like no one could survive. Though, some will. Some will be taken alive in judgment and some will remain alive on the earth to enter into the Millennium.

One generation is saved from this period of wrath of seven years on the earth, perhaps it will be our generation. If Jesus came today, we would go to Heaven with Him and then the seven-year Tribulation will begin on the earth. Many at that time will believe the message of the one hundred and forty-four thousand in Revelation 7. Multitudes will be saved from every tribe, people, tongue, and nations. Many will be martyred. Some will survive this time and enter into the Millennium. At the end of the Tribulation, Jesus will come, riding on a white horse and taking one in judgment while another will be left to enter into His Kingdom. We have seen there are no signs for the Rapture; it is a signless, timeless event. There will be a multitude of signs for the Revelation. God's Word reveals these in detail in the Book of Revelation, chapters 4-19. There are twenty-one judgments under the seals, trumpets, and vials.

There are no signs for the Rapture and a multitude of signs for the Revelation (Revelation 19), and signs today are multiplying, increasing in rapidity and intensity. All signs point to the Revelation (Revelation 19). Then we must conclude that the Second Advent of Christ riding on the white horse coming with His armies from Heaven is very near. Because this appearing is seven years after the Rapture, the Rapture itself must be much nearer (seven years nearer than the Revelation). Since the signs point to events seven years after the Rapture, and these signs are beginning to increase, then the Rapture (which takes place seven years before) must be knocking at the door. Even though there are no signs for the Rapture, I've opened the door of my heart to Jesus Christ, and He will come for me. I am *Rapture ready* (1 Thessalonians 4:13-18). Are you?

At the great triumph, Jesus is coming back as King of kings and Lord of lords. He will put down all His enemies. He is going to deliver the nation of Israel from the nations of the world. He will fulfill His covenants to Israel. Jesus will also set up His Kingdom on the earth for one thousand years. His coming will be bodily, personal, and visible. Jesus Christ will come again! Believers will come with Him and will co-reign with Him during this age. Isaiah 24:23 bears repeating, "The moon will be dismayed, the sun ashamed; for the LORD Almighty will reign on Mount Zion and in Jerusalem, and before its elders—with great glory."

Now let's look at the Millennium, the great ten centuries.

Note: A great resource on the subject matter of this chapter is the work by Mike Evans, *The Return*.

SIX

The Great Ten Centuries

"In that day I will restore David's fallen shelter—I will repair its broken walls and restore its ruins—and will rebuild it as it used to be, so that they may possess the remnant of Edom and all the nations that bear my name, declares the LORD, who will do these things." "The days are coming," declares the LORD, "when the reaper will be overtaken by the plowman and the planter by the one treading grapes. New wine will drip from the mountains and flow from all the hills, and I will bring my people Israel back from exile. They will rebuild the ruined cities and live in them. They will plant vineyards and drink their wine; they will make gardens and eat their fruit. I will plant Israel in their own land, never again to be uprooted from the land I have given them," says the LORD your God." (Amos 9:11-15)

The minor prophet Amos speaks of this period in graphic terms. His words are optimistic. That is why we are looking at optimistic prophecy. One day God will have His Day, His Say, and His Way. Satan thinks He has thwarted God's plan of the ages. However, in chapters six, seven, and eight of this book, we will see the conflict of the ages end. The conflict started in Heaven before God created the physical universe. God had created the spiritual universe with an innumerable company of angels. Lucifer, the anointed cherub, was God's crowning point of His creation, but he led a rebellion against God in Heaven and one-third of the angelic host followed Him. Jesus said that He saw Satan fall from Heaven (Luke 10:18). During the Millennium, God will start over with righteousness and peace like a river flowing over all the earth. We begin now to describe the great ten centuries.

I believe that both philosophy and history at some place must come to grips with the question, "Is history moving toward the ultimate goal?" I believe it is. Does history make sense? I believe it does. I believe Pre-millennialism provides a biblical and rational philosophy of history, an explanation of history. I believe that Pre-millennialism answers the question, "Is there a future for Israel?" Yes, there is. I believe that philosophy and history centered in the Word of God is optimistic prophecy. God isn't finished with His chosen people, Israel. God isn't finished with you or me. God isn't finished with Israel just because the prophetic clock for her has stopped. The clock is not irrevocably broken. Paul says in Romans 11:11-12,

Again I ask: Did they stumble so as to fall beyond recovery? Not at all! Rather, because of their transgression, salvation has come to the Gentiles to make Israel envious. But if their transgression means riches for the world, and their loss means riches for the Gentiles, how much greater riches will their full inclusion bring!

God is going to start that clock ticking once more! God will deal with His people again. Romans, chapter 11, would be a great read at this point.

The Millennium is the period of one thousand years of the visible, earthly reign of Jesus Christ, who, after His Second Advent, the great triumph, will establish His reign upon this earth (Luke 1:31-33), will fulfill during this period the covenant promises to Israel, will bring the whole world to a knowledge of God, and will lift the curse from creation. I disagree with "Replacement Theology" that is just the opposite. It teaches that the covenants are being fulfilled in the Church today. God, they say, does not have any plan for Israel in the future. The Church is the fulfillment of God's great plan of redemption. Israel rejected Jesus Christ and now God's blessing is on the Church. However, the Scriptures teach that *Gentile believers* have been grafted in to the vine of Israel (Romans 11:17-21). Praise God! I don't like the term "Replacement Theology" because it represents a teaching contrary to the Word of God. I have covered many Scriptures teaching just the opposite. I will continue to show from the Scriptures, especially in this chapter, God's great plan and future for His chosen people, Israel.

How is the word *Millennium* termed in the Word of God? You will not find the word Millennium in God's Word. It is Latin and means a thousand years. The Christian Church has coined this word to refer to this thousand year reign of Jesus Christ on this earth. The duration for one thousand years is seen in Revelation 20:1-7 where a thousand years appears six times. The extent of the Millennium is universal in two ways, physical and spiritual, as seen in Zechariah 14:9, Isaiah 2:1-4, and Daniel 7:13-14.

There are several designations for the Millennium in the Word of God. Jesus spoke about it. The Apostle Paul spoke about it. The Apostle Peter spoke about it. Hear Jesus speak in Matthew 19:28, "Jesus said to them, 'Truly I tell you, at the renewal of all things, when the Son of Man sits on his glorious throne, you who have followed me will also sit on twelve thrones, judging the twelve tribes of Israel.'" "Renewal" speaks of a rejuvenation that will take place in the future when the curse placed on the earth will be lifted. Jesus was speaking to His disciples. Jesus used his favorite title for Himself, the Son of Man. Jesus is referring to the glorious time when He will be reigning from Jerusalem seated upon David's throne. Jesus speaks of the "renewal of all things," which is the regeneration. Regeneration in the Greek means to produce anew. The earth is going to go through what we call spiritually "to be born again." The earth will be physically "born again."

Another designation for the Millennium in Scripture is found in Acts 3. The context is after the Day of Pentecost. Peter and John were headed to the temple around 3:00 p.m. for prayer. On the way, they encountered a lame man. Peter told him to rise up and walk in the name of Jesus Christ. He leaped up, stood, and walked and entered the temple with Peter and John, walking, leaping, and praising God. Peter then preached in Solomon's Portico in the temple to the crowd gathered there to pray. Peter told them he had not healed the lame man but that it was in Jesus' name he was healed. Peter then told them that they had delivered up Jesus and denied Him before Pilate. They denied the Holy and Just One. They killed the Prince of Life. God raised him up. Peter and the other disciples were witnesses. It was only in the matchless name of Jesus that the lame man was made strong. Peter continues by saying in Acts 3:17-21,

> Now, fellow Israelites, I know that you acted in ignorance, as did your leaders. But this is how God fulfilled what he foretold through all the prophets, saying that his Messiah would suffer. Repent, then, and turn to God, so that your sins may be wiped out, that times of refreshing may come from the Lord, and that he may send the Messiah, who has been appointed for you—even Jesus. Heaven must receive him until the time comes for God to restore everything, as he promised long ago through his holy prophets.

There will be theocracy on earth; a society ruled by God. The great ten centuries will be a theocracy, ruled by Jesus Christ from the throne of David in Jerusalem; the rule of God over men. The "times of refreshing" will come when Jesus comes to set up His Kingdom on Earth. Today, Heaven must receive Him until God's timing for the restoration of all things. It will literally take place. Remember, at the Rapture He comes in the air to the first Heaven, the terrestrial Heaven where the birds fly. There He will catch up His Bride, His Church. His feet will not touch the earth. We will pass through the first Heaven into the second Heaven where the planets and stars exist, then into the third Heaven, the throne of God, the very Presence of the Almighty Himself. The times of refreshing and restoration of all things will not come at the Rapture. They will happen at the Revelation of Jesus Christ. We saw the great triumph in the last chapter. Jesus the Conqueror at His Second Advent will lift the curse from creation. He will restore all things marred by evil and sin.

Isaiah 9:6-7 reveals to us Jesus' two comings,

> For to us a child is born, to us a son is given, and the government will be on his shoulders. And he will be called Wonderful Counselor, Mighty God, Everlasting Father, Prince of Peace. Of the greatness of his government and peace there will be no end. He will reign on David's throne and over his kingdom, establishing and upholding it with justice and righteousness from that time on and forever. The zeal of the LORD Almighty will accomplish this.

Isaiah in prophecy speaks of a Child being born and a Son being given. God gave His Son (John 3:16) and the Child was born of the virgin, Mary, conceived by the Holy Spirit of God. Jesus Christ is both God and Man. He is the Theanthropic Person, the God-Man, Son of God and Son of Man. Jesus is one hundred percent God and one hundred percent man. The sum does not equal two hundred percent, but one hundred percent; one Person with two natures, divine and human. Praise God for the first advent of Jesus Christ (Galatians 4:4)! God's plan was for His Son to enter the container of a human being, to be like us in every way, yet without sin (John 1:14). Was it true at His first coming that He ruled government and ushered in peace? Did He rule from the throne of David in His Kingdom, in judgment and justice? Was the world's government upon His shoulders? Did the zeal of the Lord of hosts perform this at His first advent? The answer is "No" for all questions. It is for another time and age called the great ten centuries.

It will be accomplished at His Revelation when His feet will touch the earth and the whole world will be brought to the knowledge of God. The knowledge of God will permeate the whole earth. Remember Zechariah 14:9, "The LORD will be king over the whole earth. On that day there will be one LORD, and his name the only name." Jesus did not reign over David's Throne in Jerusalem at His first coming. He was rejected, tortured, and crucified. He went through all that for us, enduring the cross and despising the shame (Hebrews 12:2). *All for us!* The Head of government in the Millennium will be the King, Jesus Christ. Jeremiah spoke about the Branch of Righteousness; hear him now in Jeremiah 23:5-6,

> "The days are coming," declares the LORD, "when I will raise up for David a righteous Branch, a King who will reign wisely and do what is just and right in the land. In his days Judah will be saved and Israel will live in safety. This is the name by which he will be called: The LORD Our Righteous Savior."

The center of government during the Millennium will be at Jerusalem. It will be a political entity. The Head of the government is our King, Jesus Christ (Jeremiah 23:5 and Isaiah 9:6-7). Isaiah 4:3-5 tells us about the center of government,

> Those who are left in Zion, who remain in Jerusalem, will be called holy, all who are recorded among the living in Jerusalem. The Lord will wash away the filth of the women of Zion; he will cleanse the bloodstains from Jerusalem by a spirit of judgment and a spirit of fire. Then the LORD will create over all of Mount Zion and over those who assemble there a cloud of smoke by day and a glow of flaming fire by night; over everything the glory will be a canopy. See also Isaiah 2:3 and Zechariah 14:4.

The groups of people related to the Millennium will be three. First, Israel will be gathered to her land and turned to the Lord. The Palestinian Covenant promised to Israel will be fulfilled. Then the nations (Gentiles) will be subjects of the King. Third, the Church of Jesus Christ will be married to Christ, His Bride. We will co-reign with Him during this period of time. We saw at the great trumpeting translation (the Rapture) that we will always be with the Lord. I'm a literalist. To me, always means always. Wherever Jesus Christ is, that is where His Church will be. Whatever Jesus Christ is doing is what His Church will be doing.

What is the spiritual character of the Millennium? What do I mean by that? The Millennium will not be spiritualized, not an allegory. It will be literal, but very spiritual in character and nature. It will be a Kingdom characterized by obedience, righteousness, holiness, truth, joy, peace, knowledge, health, and fullness of the Holy Spirit. All these and more will be manifested in the Millennium. Mankind will be saved precisely as we are saved today, trusting in Jesus Christ by faith alone as their Lord and Savior, by God's grace, on the grounds of the death of Christ which satisfies the righteous demands of God the Father. The Apostle John wrote it this way in 1 John 2:2, "He is the atoning sacrifice for our sins, and not only for ours but also for the sins of the whole world." Other versions use the word propitiation. Propitiation means God's wrath has been averted by the atoning sacrifice of Jesus. The Father is completely satisfied with the death of His Son. Propitiation for all, for the whole world, past, present, and future, is only found in Jesus. Jesus satisfied the righteous demands of the Father; He averted the Father's wrath from us, because without Jesus we are abiding in God's wrath. Jesus spoke of this, "For God did not send his Son into the world to condemn the world, but to save the world through him. Whoever believes in him is not condemned, but whoever does not believe stands condemned already because they have not believed in the name of God's one and only Son" (John 3:17-18). There will finally be a true Theocracy on the earth. Jesus will reign from David's throne in Jerusalem.

One main purpose for the Millennium (why it is necessary) is to lift the curse from creation. God will redeem the earth from the curse imposed upon it. God created all things good, even very good. "God saw all that he had made, and it was very good. And there was evening, and there was morning—the sixth day" (Genesis 1:31). Creation was defiled by man's sin (Genesis 3). The Apostle Paul tells us in Romans 8:18-25,

> I consider that our present sufferings are not worth comparing with the glory that will be revealed in us. For the creation waits in eager expectation for the children of God to be revealed. For the creation was subjected to frustration, not by its own choice, but by the will of the

> one who subjected it, in hope that the creation itself will be liberated from its bondage to decay and brought into the freedom and glory of the children of God. We know that the whole creation has been groaning as in the pains of childbirth right up to the present time. Not only so, but we ourselves, who have the firstfruits of the Spirit, groan inwardly as we wait eagerly for our adoption to sonship, the redemption of our bodies. For in this hope we were saved. But hope that is seen is no hope at all. Who hopes for what they already have? But if we hope for what we do not yet have, we wait for it patiently.

God, as recorded in Genesis 3, put a curse upon the earth because of man's sin. God put a curse upon Adam. God put a curse upon Eve. The word curse means to place disapproval upon; God put a strong disapproval upon the earth, a curse, because of sin. Jesus is going to lift the curse from creation. This did not happen at His first coming. In fact, during His public ministry He cursed a fig tree. Symbolically, He was putting disapproval upon Israel because she did not recognize God's day of visitation. God came in the form of man, a Jewish man. Jesus was not received (John 1:10). As we have seen, the earth will be born again at His great triumph at the end of the Tribulation period when He comes to establish His Kingdom on the earth. God's disapproval that started in Genesis 3 will be lifted.

Other purposes include God's original design for man: to effect the establishment of a perfect divine Theocracy upon the earth; to fulfill God's eternal covenant with Israel; to provide a final test for fallen humanity, and to make a full manifestation of the glory of Christ in the Kingdom He rules.

What is the Millennial Kingdom based upon? It is based upon the covenants of the Old Testament. Before we look at the four specific unconditional covenants promised to Israel in the Old Testament, we need to look at a few others. In the *Edenic Covenant* (conditional covenant based upon Adam's obedience), Adam was promised that eating the fruit of the tree of the knowledge of good and evil would result in death, and obedience would bring life. He ate. His indigestion has affected us all. God provided the cure for this spiritual indigestion that resulted in death. In the *Adamic Covenant* (unconditional covenant based only on the faithfulness of God), God promised to restore the kingdom through an offspring of Eve who would defeat the serpent and his offspring (Genesis 3:15). This is the *protoevangelium*, the first picture of God providing the One and Only Savior from the seed of the woman. Genesis 3:15 says, "And I will put enmity between you and the woman, and between your offspring and hers; he will crush your head, and you will strike his heel." Paul would say in Galatians 3:16, "The promises were spoken to Abraham and to his *seed*. Scripture does not say "and to *seeds*," meaning many people, but "and to your *seed*," meaning one person, who is *Christ*." When Adam turned over the title deed of dominion and authority over the earth to Satan, the world was cursed, death began, sorrow increased, and enmity, strife, division, and contention ruled the day. Christ conquered Satan and his offspring at Calvary. Through His death, He regained the title deed to the earth and the full display of that will be seen during the Millennium when Satan will be bound for one thousand years. In the *Noahic Covenant* (unconditional covenant based only on the faithfulness of God in Genesis 9:16 where it is called an everlasting covenant), God has promised never to destroy the earth again by a deluge and gave the rainbow as a sign and seal of His promise. Next time the world will be destroyed by fire as we will see in a future chapter, "The Great Timeless Forever."

The Millennium is based upon the faithfulness of God and His Word. It is based upon the covenant God who is Jehovah. It is based upon God's own Word, His Covenant, His Name, and His Oath. God has exalted His Word above His Name (Psalm 138:2). God is going to keep His Word. God gave four unconditional covenants to His people in the Old Testament. When I say unconditional covenants, I mean there are no strings attached. God's faithfulness is in view. God and His Word are steadfast and unchanging. They are not based upon the faithfulness and obedience of man. These covenants do not depend upon God's people for their fulfillment. The nation of Israel sinned over and over again. They broke another covenant called the law. The law that God gave at Mount Sinai was more than just the Ten Commandments. It was all the law found in the Pentateuch, the first five books of God's Word, written by Moses. There were so many statutes, decrees, and ordinances that the nation of Israel was to live by from the law. In the *Mosaic* or *Sinaitic Covenant* (Exodus 19:5-6), God provided the law to Israel, obedience to which would bring blessing or cursing in the Promised Land (Exodus 19:5). James speaks loudly here in James 2:10, "For whoever keeps the whole law and yet stumbles at just one point is guilty of breaking all of it." God gave the law as a schoolmaster, the tutor, to bring us to a saving knowledge of Jesus Christ. The law was to point us to the Savior. The law was righteous, holy, and good, but it could not save. God provided the Savior, the Lamb of God, the Son of God. Israel was indeed a stubborn and stiff-necked people, not unlike us. They could not keep the law, nor can we. Thank God for grace, yesterday, today, and forever. In contrast, the four unconditional covenants God gave to Israel, the Abrahamic, Palestinian, Davidic, and New Covenants are not based upon man's obedience; they are based upon the faithfulness of our covenant-keeping God. The basis of Pre-millennialism is the four unconditional covenants of God.

The Abrahamic Covenant promised to God's people, Israel, permanent existence as a nation and permanent possession of the Land, The Promised Land (Genesis 12:1-7; 13:14-17; 17:7-10). God promised to use Abraham and his offspring to be a channel of blessing to all the world. He has promised this through His seed, Jesus Christ. The extent of the Land is found in Genesis 15:18; Exodus 23:31; Deuteronomy 1:6-8; Deuteronomy 11:24; Joshua 1:1-8; 2 Samuel 8:3; 1 Kings 4:21. This covenant was given 2,000 years before Christ.

The Palestinian Covenant promised Israel restoration to, and permanent resettlement in, the land of Palestine (Deuteronomy 30:1-10). God's ultimate restoration will be Israel as a believing nation in her own land after their removal for disobedience. She will be so blessed to be in the Millennium with Jesus Christ, her God. God confirmed this covenant with Isaac in Genesis 26:1-6 and Jacob in Genesis 28:10-22. See also Amos 9:13-15 and Joel 3:20-21. This covenant was also given 2,000 years before Christ.

The Davidic Covenant promised to Israel a "seed" forever, a "throne" forever, and a "kingdom" forever (2 Samuel 7:4-17; Psalm

89:3-4; 19-37). God promised David that his offspring would sit on the throne of Israel forever and that the ultimate ruler of the nation of Israel and the world would come from David's line. This was said of Jesus in the New Testament. Luke records,

> In the sixth month of Elizabeth's pregnancy, God sent the angel Gabriel to Nazareth, a town in Galilee, to a virgin pledged to be married to a man named Joseph, a descendant of David. The virgin's name was Mary. The angel went to her and said, "Greetings, you who are highly favored! The Lord is with you." Mary was greatly troubled at his words and wondered what kind of greeting this might be. But the angel said to her, "Do not be afraid, Mary; you have found favor with God. You will conceive and give birth to a son, and you are to call him Jesus. He will be great and will be called the Son of the Most High. The Lord God will give him the throne of his father David, and he will reign over Jacob's descendants forever; his kingdom will never end. (Luke 1:26-33)

The Davidic Covenant was given 1,000 years before Christ. The angel Gabriel foretold the birth of Jesus Christ to Mary. It would be her child ("the seed of the woman") who would be the fulfillment of this prophecy.

The New Covenant, finally, promised to Israel a "new heart" (regeneration) by which to enjoy the first three covenants (Jeremiah 31:31-37; Romans 11:11; 25-27; Hebrews 8:8-12; 10:11-18). God promised in the New Covenant that He would give Israel forgiveness and a new heart to obey Him so that they would be able to enjoy the promise of their ultimate restoration to the Promised Land with the ultimate rule under one King. This would be forever. This covenant was given 600 years before Christ.

See Appendix I: *Peace in the Middle East*, by Senator James M. Inhofe from Oklahoma. It is a Senate Floor Statement given March 4, 2002. Senator Inhofe gives seven reasons (proofs) that Israel has the right to their land. Israel does have the right to the Promised Land. It is given to her by God Himself.

The Bible is a Jewish Book. Salvation is of the Jews. Jesus was a Jew. Salvation has come to the Gentiles through the Jewish Messiah, the Christ, Jesus. John 4:22 says, "You Samaritans worship what you do not know; we worship what we do know, for salvation is from the Jews." Jesus Himself spoke those words to the woman at the well at Sychar in Samaria. Paul shares these verses with us in the Book of Romans, 11:12, "But if their transgression means riches for the world, and their loss means riches for the Gentiles, how much greater riches will their full inclusion bring!" and Romans 11:25-26,

> I do not want you to be ignorant of this mystery, brothers and sisters, so that you may not be conceited: Israel has experienced a hardening in part until the full number of the Gentiles has come in, and in this way all Israel will be saved. As it is written: "The deliverer will come from Zion; he will turn godlessness away from Jacob."

God has given an oath, His Word, and His promise to His chosen people, Israel. He will fulfill what He has said in the "fullness of time," just as He did at Christ's first advent (Galatians 4:4). God is the only One who knows when that set time will come.

The literal character of the Millennium and the Kingdom of Jesus Christ established on the earth are part of our "Blessed Hope." Scriptures speak loudly to the kingdom being established on "this" earth (Zechariah 14:9; Jeremiah 23:5; Daniel 2:35; 44-45; Psalm 2:8). We see the inception of the Millennium vividly described in the Book of Revelation, chapters 19 and 20.

Conditions present during the Millennium are numerous. Picture the Garden of Eden again on the earth, with perfect peace and righteousness. Age will even be different during the Millennial Age. "Never again will there be in it an infant who lives but a few days, or an old man who does not live out his years; the one who dies at a hundred will be thought a mere child; the one who fails to reach a hundred will be considered accursed" (Isaiah 65:20). There will be longevity of life with pre-flood ages. The antediluvian age on earth was in the hundreds of years. It will be once more during the great ten centuries. At this time, the Bride of Christ will be in resurrected or raptured glorified bodies. Those believers who make it all the way through the Great Tribulation will be preserved physically. Jesus said in Matthew 24:13, "but the one who stands firm to the end will be saved." Those who endure to the end of the Great Tribulation will be in bodies like we have today, physical and mortal. They will be the ones who will have children with sinful natures. Many will live a long time while others will even die during the great ten centuries. Everyone at the start of the Millennial Kingdom will be saved (unbelievers taken in judgment of the sheep and the goats), even as everyone at the start of the Great Tribulation will be lost (believers raptured). I believe a few minutes into the Millennium babies will be born, many babies. They will have unregenerate, Adamic natures. Mankind is saved during the Millennium precisely as they are saved today, by God's grace alone through faith in our Lord Jesus Christ. Those who are born during this time will be in mortal bodies subject to death.

Jesus will be reigning during this period. We, the Bride of Christ, will co-reign with Him, and the nations who come out of the Great Tribulation will be subjects to the King. Israel will be gathered to the land forever, never to be dispersed again. All this is pictured in type on the Mount of Transfiguration (Mt. Horeb or Mt. Carmel). Peter, James, and John ascended the mount together with Jesus. Jesus was transfigured into His majestic body of glory, the Shekinah glory. The three disciples were in their mortal bodies while Moses and Elijah appeared speaking to Jesus about His death on Calvary that would be accomplished at Jerusalem. Moses and Elijah were in spiritual bodies suited for the Millennium. Combining the spiritual bodies with mortal physical bodies apparent at the transfiguration of Jesus, you have what the Millennial Kingdom will look like. King Jesus will be reigning over those who are in their resurrected, glorified bodies (spiritual bodies) and those in their mortal physical bodies. We will co-inhabit with those who come out of the Great Tribulation in mortal bodies, as we will be in resurrected, raptured glorified bodies. And, greatest of all, we will be with Jesus Christ. What a beautiful picture!

Isaiah wrote seven centuries before Jesus Christ in Isaiah 65:17-25,

"See, I will create new heavens and a new earth. The former things will not be remembered, nor will they come to mind. But be glad and rejoice forever in what I will create, for I will create Jerusalem to be a delight and its people a joy. I will rejoice over Jerusalem and take delight in my people; the sound of weeping and of crying will be heard in it no more. Never again will there be in it an infant who lives but a few days, or an old man who does not live out his years; the one who dies at a hundred will be thought a mere child; the one who fails to reach a hundred will be considered accursed. They will build houses and dwell in them; they will plant vineyards and eat their fruit. No longer will they build houses and others live in them, or plant and others eat. For as the days of a tree, so will be the days of my people; my chosen ones will long enjoy the work of their hands. They will not labor in vain, nor will they bear children doomed to misfortune; for they will be a people blessed by the LORD, they and their descendants with them. Before they call I will answer; while they are still speaking I will hear. The wolf and the lamb will feed together, and the lion will eat straw like the ox, and dust will be the serpent's food. They will neither harm nor destroy on all my holy mountain," says the LORD.

People will be born during this time, and the longevity of life will be more than threescore and ten or even fourscore. People will live hundreds and hundreds of years. Someone's age at one hundred will be considered a mere youth. Methuselah has the record to date, nine hundred and sixty-nine years, thirty-nine years more than Adam. Perhaps Methuselah's record will be broken! Time will tell.

Another condition that will take place is the reverse of the Tower of Babel. Jehovah confused the one language and one speech that existed after the flood at the Tower of Babel. Many languages appeared. The Towel of Babel became babble. The people were dispersed all over the world (Genesis 11:9). During the Millennium, people addressing one another will speak with one voice, one language. The barrier of many tongues will be eliminated. Zephaniah 3:9 shouts, "Then I will purify the lips of the peoples, that all of them may call on the name of the LORD and serve him shoulder to shoulder." There will be no miscommunication and no misunderstanding. God will provide one language for His creation. Think about that; the whole world calling on the name of the Lord in unison, in the same language. Everyone will serve the Lord shoulder to shoulder, giving allegiance to our Lord Jesus Christ.

A third condition present during the Millennium is a change in agriculture. There will be economic prosperity during this age. Micah 4:1-4 says,

> In the last days the mountain of the LORD's temple will be established as the highest of the mountains; it will be exalted above the hills, and peoples will stream to it. Many nations will come and say, "Come, let us go up to the mountain of the LORD, to the temple of the God of Jacob. He will teach us his ways, so that we may walk in his paths." The law will go out from Zion, the word of the LORD from Jerusalem. He will judge between many peoples and will settle disputes for strong nations far and wide. They will beat their swords into plowshares and their spears into pruning hooks. Nation will not take up sword against nation, nor will they train for war anymore. Everyone will sit under their own vine and under their own fig tree, and no one will make them afraid, for the LORD Almighty has spoken.

Read the parallel passage in Isaiah 2:1-4. The weapons of swords and spears are weapons of warfare. They will be replaced by implements of agriculture; plowshares, and pruning hooks. Also read Joel 3:9-21. This is a contrasting picture. The minor prophet Joel speaks of a time when the implements of agriculture, plowshares and pruning hooks, will be turned into weapons of war; swords, and spears. Joel gives a prophecy concerning a different time period. Joel prophesies at a time during the Great Tribulation when there will be war. Micah speaks of a time when they will not train for war.

When Jesus Christ comes at the great triumph (Revelation 19) to set up His Kingdom of peace and righteousness, then, and only then, will weapons of war become implements of agriculture. There will be economic prosperity and a bumper crop. The ground will produce a hundred-fold.

The minor prophet Amos speaks of the day when Israel will be restored and never dispersed again. Israel will be dispersed again during the Tribulation, but in the Millennium she will enjoy God's covenant blessings. The prophecy in Amos 9:13-15 speaks volumes. The cycles of growth, the seasons for growing crops, also change during the Millennium. There is no poverty. There is plenty of food and economic prosperity when the curse on creation is lifted. The ground is no longer under God's curse and man will know the fullness of God's provision from the ground, vine, and tree. Indeed, the mountains shall drip with sweet, new wine. Micah says that. Isaiah says that. Amos says that. Everything is contingent upon Amos 9:15. Israel's existence as a nation is guaranteed by God Himself, and she will be planted by Jehovah in the Land promised to Abraham and his descendants. God's promise is that they will never be uprooted from their land again. Joel says, "Judah will be inhabited forever and Jerusalem through all generations" (Joel 3:20).

Let's look at one more point to the Millennium: its conclusion. After the conclusion of the Millennium, between the Millennium and the eternal state, *four* specific events will take place. See Revelation 20:7 to Revelation 21:1. The four events are the release and revolt of Satan, the purging of creation, the judgment of the final impenitent (The Great White Throne Judgment seen in the next chapter), and the creation of the New Heavens and New Earth that take us to the eternal state—the great timeless forever. I believe these four specific events will take place rapidly.

Revelation 20:7-10 says,

> When the thousand years are over, Satan will be released from his prison and will go out to deceive the nations in the four corners of the earth—Gog and Magog—and to gather them for battle. In number, they are like the sand on the seashore. They marched across the breadth of the

> earth and surrounded the camp of God's people, the city he loves. But fire came down from heaven and devoured them. And the devil, who deceived them, was thrown into the lake of burning sulfur where the beast and the false prophet had been thrown. They will be tormented day and night for ever and ever.

On Satan's part, it is one final attempt to overthrow the Divine Theocracy. Theocracy is the rule of God over any society, over angels, the host of Heaven, and over man. Lucifer tried to overthrow the Divine Theocracy in Heaven before God created the physical universe (Isaiah 14 and Ezekiel 28). He tried on the earth in the Garden of Eden with Adam and Eve (Genesis 3). He will even fail to overthrow the rule of God in Heaven when he and his angels war with Michael and his angels during the Great Tribulation (Revelation 12). There is a major war that will break out in Heaven. Satan (the dragon) and his angels will not prevail, and no place will be found for them in heaven any longer. They will be forced out of Heaven. The great, fiery red dragon and his cohorts will be kicked out of Heaven, cast out forever. Concerning the initial rebellion of Lucifer in Heaven, Jesus, during His three and one-half years of public ministry, spoke of this rebellion. "He replied, 'I saw Satan fall like lightning from heaven'" (Luke 10:18).

On Satan's part, too, it is one final demonstration to show the corruption of the human heart, man's depraved nature. For one thousand years, it has been the "Garden of Eden" on earth. Man has had a perfect environment. You can change mankind's external circumstances and situations, but unless the human heart is changed through repentance and regeneration, it does no good. The nations will come to Jesus during the great ten centuries, and He will settle disputes among nations far and wide. The nations will give their public and outward allegiance to Jesus Christ, the King over the whole earth, in a Divine Theocracy. However, many people have not been born again. When Satan is released from prison, the bottomless pit, has he been reformed or rehabilitated? No! He is up to his old tricks. He will deceive the nations once more. He has been in the bottomless pit or the abyss under lock and key. He takes people captive to do his will (2 Timothy 2:26). It started with the first Adam (Genesis 3) and it will end with the *Last Adam*, Jesus Christ (1 Corinthians 15:45). Praise God, Jesus, is the Last Adam! He is the First and the Last. He has the keys of Hades and Death (Revelation 1:18). Satan means the enemy. He is the enemy of God and man. He will continue to be our enemy. Satan is also the devil. Devil means the deceiver who destroys. He is called the angel of the bottomless pit, whose name in Hebrew is *Abaddon* and in Greek his name is *Apollyon,* both meaning the Destroyer, the one who brings destruction (Revelation 9:11).

He will be released and will deceive once more. He deceives today, and we are his enemy. After his release in Revelation 20, he wages war again. He could not wage war during the great ten centuries because he, the roaring lion, could not walk about on earth seeking whom he could devour, because he was caged. Upon his release, he will gather a vast worldwide army whose number is as the sand of the sea. Once more mankind will beat their plowshares into swords and their pruning hooks into spears. When this vast army is gathered, the implements of agriculture will again be turned into implements of war. How tragic!

Where do these people come from? As we have seen, many children will be born during the Millennial Kingdom. These children will have a sinful nature, inherent from birth because of Adam's original sin. These children will live long lives and give outward allegiance to Jesus Christ. Many will be born again, but others will not. Satan will gather his army from these unbelievers and march on the beloved city, Jerusalem, where Jesus Christ has had His headquarters for one thousand years. God allows fire to fall from Heaven, and it devours them. Then the devil, the deceiver, will be cast into the lake of fire and brimstone (final Hell, Gehenna) where the Beast and False Prophet are (Revelation 19:20). Praise God! The Beast and False Prophet have been captured and are the first humans to be assigned to Gehenna. They have been thrown alive into the lake of fire, of burning sulfur. Satan, along with these two evil men, will be tormented day and night forever and ever (Revelation 20:10). Are you applauding? Are you shouting Hallelujah? Satan is eternally defeated, banned for eternity from the presence of God and

His people. The conflict of the ages that has been raging between Lucifer and God will finally be over. Praise God!

After the release and revolt of Satan, the purging of creation and the judgment of the final impenitent (The Great White Throne Judgment seen in the next chapter), will occur at the same time. The creation of the New Heavens and the New Earth will take us to the "Eternal State." The "Eternal State" will be studied in this book's final chapter on The Great Timeless Forever. I believe all the four specific events will take place rapidly as we will see in the next two chapters.

Note: A resource on the subject matter of this chapter is the work by Arnold G. Fruchtenbaum, *The Footsteps of the Messiah*.

SEVEN

The Great White Throne Judgment

> Then I saw a great white throne and him who was seated on it. The earth and the heavens fled from his presence, and there was no place for them. And I saw the dead, great and small, standing before the throne, and books were opened. Another book was opened, which is the book of life. The dead were judged according to what they had done as recorded in the books. The sea gave up the dead that were in it, and death and Hades gave up the dead that were in them, and each person was judged according to what they had done. Then death and Hades were thrown into the lake of fire. The lake of fire is the second death. Anyone whose name was not found written in the book of life was thrown into the lake of fire. (Revelation 20:11-15)

John speaks with God's authority in Revelation 20:11-15. God, at the timing of the Great White Throne Judgment, will purge His creation. God said it, I believe it, and that's good enough for me. God will do it, not man. It is part of the Day of the Lord, the Day of God. I'm looking for the home of righteousness. The Old Testament teaches that the earth will abide forever; Jerusalem will be inhabited and abide forever, and Judah will abide forever. The earth will be destroyed, but not annihilated, when God purges His creation. The heavens and earth will not go out of existence. The old heavens and earth will be purged by fire and God from the ashes will create New Heavens and a New Earth. The author of Hebrews teaches us about this in Hebrews 1:10-12,

> He also says, "In the beginning, Lord, you laid the foundations of the earth, and the heavens are the work of your hands. They will perish, but you remain; they will all wear out like a garment. You will roll them up like a robe; like a garment they will be changed. But you remain the same, and your years will never end."

The author of Hebrews quotes Psalm 102:25-27. God will send the old heavens and earth to the cleaners! Think of an old garment or cloak that He will fold up, and it will be changed.

Why will God have to purge His creation? After the Millennium, Satan is back on the earth bringing destruction. The earth is polluted again. The release and revolt of Satan are seen in Revelation 20:7-10. Our enemy is once and for all confined to the "lake of burning sulfur." His reign of ruin, destruction, stealing, killing, lying, and destroying is over. Why is Satan released? On Satan's part, he has one final attempt to overthrow the Divine Theocracy. On God's part, He gives one final test to demonstrate the corruption of the human heart (man's nature).

Up until the mid-point of the Tribulation, Satan has had access to Heaven (Job, chapters 1 and 2). In Revelation 12, we have seen that Satan will lose the war with Michael and his angels. Satan will be cast out of Heaven with his angels and thrown down to the earth. His pollution includes the first, second, and third Heaven. All will be changed. When will this take place? It will take place after the close of the Millennium. The purging of creation and the Great White Throne Judgment take place simultaneously. The Apostle John says, "Then I saw a great white throne and him who was seated on it. The earth and the heavens fled from his presence, and there was no place for them" (Revelation 20:11). "The earth and the heavens fled from his presence" refers to the purging of creation (Hebrews

1:10-12; Psalm 102:25-27). God has reserved the earth for fire until the day of judgment and perdition of ungodly men. This is the judgment of the final impenitent. The Great White Throne Judgment is the Supreme Court of the universe for the final impenitent, all the wicked dead of all ages. Jesus still speaks clearly today as He did during His public ministry, "Do not be afraid of those who kill the body but cannot kill the soul. Rather, be afraid of the One who can destroy both soul and body in hell" (Matthew 10:28).

The Apostle John reveals to us what has been revealed to him in Revelation 20:11-15. The day of judgment and perdition of ungodly men refers to the Great White Throne Judgment. It is the judgment of the lost of all ages. It will take place after the close of the Millennium.

Who judges? Jesus Christ will judge. Jesus said in John 5:22-23, "Moreover, the Father judges no one, but has entrusted all judgment to the Son, that all may honor the Son just as they honor the Father. Whoever does not honor the Son does not honor the Father, who sent him." God the Father has entrusted all judgment to His Son. The Apostle Paul agrees, "For he has set a day when he will judge the world with justice by the man he has appointed. He has given proof of this to everyone by raising him from the dead" (Acts 17:31).

John saw the Great White Throne and Him who was seated on it. From Scripture, we know that he saw Jesus. At this moment, the earth and Heaven will flee from His presence, and there will be found no place for them. What is happening here? What is taking place? Again, it is the purging of creation.

John continues and says he saw the dead stand before God. Who are subjects of this judgment? They are the great and small who have been resurrected to stand in judgment before God. Scripture is replete with references that God is no respecter of persons. Those present will be the rich and famous, the infamous, and those with lowly stations in this life. They are the great and small who rejected God's offer of salvation by God's grace through faith in His Son, Jesus Christ. Cain will be there. He was the first to go to Sheol (Hades). Noah's unbelieving generation who scoffed at him while the ark was being prepared will be there. Ahab and Jezebel will be there. Herod the Great will be there. Pontus Pilate will be there. Judas Iscariot will be there. So many, many more will be there, standing outside God's grace; the lost of all ages, all the wicked dead. Death and Hades are resurrected at this time to stand in judgment before Jesus Christ. Death or the grave claims the material part of man, the body. Hades claims the immaterial part of man, the spirit. The sea also claims the material part of man, the body. Many have been lost at sea. The sea claims the body. Read the true story of the Rich Man and Lazarus that Jesus spoke of in Luke 16:19-31. Both men were buried. Lazarus was in Abraham's bosom in rest and comfort. The rich man (Dives) was in Hades in torment. The rich man will be there at the Great White Throne Judgment. The basis of this judgment is found in the books that will be opened, and the book that God will open is the Book of Life. The other books contain the evil deeds of the wicked who deserve to be there. Their names are not written in the Book of Life. Their destiny cannot be changed. There is no hope of reversal. There is no eternal life with God for them, only eternal separation from God. That is true Hell, Gehenna, the final Hell. Jesus told his disciples not to rejoice because demons were subject to them, but rather rejoice because their names were written in heaven (Luke 10:20). There is eternal life today for all who trust Jesus Christ as Lord and Savior.

It is interesting to see another passage about the Book of Life in Philippians 4:1-4. Paul had to write the church of Philippi concerning Euodia and Syntyche and admonished them to agree in the Lord. Seemingly, they were not in harmony with one another. Paul speaks of others who also worked with him in spreading the gospel, fellow workers like Clement, all whose names were in the Book of Life, including Euodia and Syntyche. Then he told them twice to rejoice. They were to rejoice in the Lord always. When the Book of Life is opened at the Great White Throne Judgment, it will show that those standing there do not have Christ. There will be no rejoicing then. The only sin that will send you to Hell is rejection of Jesus Christ as one's personal Lord and Savior. Rejoice now in your salvation in Jesus Christ alone!

The wicked dead will be judged according to their works recorded in the books. Just think about it. God is still recording the sinful acts and deeds of men as He has done since man was created (Genesis 1). The basis of judgment is the deeds (works) of the wicked. Jude, the half-brother of our Lord Jesus Christ, speaks of depraved and doomed apostates this way in Jude, verse 15, "to judge everyone, and to convict all of them of all the ungodly acts they have committed in their ungodliness, and of all the defiant words ungodly sinners have spoken against him." The word *Him* that Jude uses refers to the Lord who is coming with ten thousands of His saints (verse 14 of Jude). The ungodly will stand before God in judgment at the Great White Throne Judgment. No one will be spared at this judgment. No one will be saved. No one will rejoice.

The results of the judgment are revealed in Revelation 20:14. Death and Hades will be cast into the lake of fire, the second death. The purpose of judgment will be fulfilled, which is to sentence the ungodly to their doom in final Hell, Gehenna, the second death. Who is already there? Revelation teaches that the Beast, the False Prophet, and Satan will already be there. They will be joined by the wicked of all ages because anyone not found written in the Book of Life will be cast into the lake of fire. "Then death and Hades were thrown into the lake of fire. The lake of fire is the second death. Anyone whose name was not found written in the book of life was thrown into the lake of fire" (Revelation 20:14-15). My heart breaks for the lost. Does yours?

I have mentioned Gehenna several times. I believe a detailed look at the four main words where the wicked are kept is warranted. First, Sheol is used thirty-one times. It refers to the underworld, the netherworld, the world of the dead. It comes from the root word in Hebrew meaning to make hollow. It literally means "a hollow place." It refers to the lowest pit; deep under the earth where the dead abide (KJV: Jonah 2:2; Job 26:6; Psalm 9:17, and Psalm 139:8). It is the only Old Testament name for the place of departed spirits.

Second, Hades is introduced in the New Testament. It is the region of departed spirits of the lost. It corresponds to Sheol of the Old Testament. Hades is a place of punishment for the disembodied dead. It is the present place of torment and punishment. In time, it is the intermediate state between the decease of the lost and doom of Gehenna. It is not the permanent region of the lost.

One day Hades will be emptied. It will be raised to stand before the Great White Throne Judgment (Revelation 20:13-14). The word is used four times in the gospels, always by the Lord Jesus Christ. It is used a total of ten times in the New Testament. Jesus gave a true story about Hades in Luke 16:19-31,

> There was a rich man who was dressed in purple and fine linen and lived in luxury every day. At his gate was laid a beggar named Lazarus, covered with sores and longing to eat what fell from the rich man's table. Even the dogs came and licked his sores. The time came when the beggar died and the angels carried him to Abraham's side. The rich man also died and was buried. In Hades, where he was in torment, he looked up and saw Abraham far away, with Lazarus by his side. So he called to him, "Father Abraham, have pity on me and send Lazarus to dip the tip of his finger in water and cool my tongue, because I am in agony in this fire." But Abraham replied, "Son, remember that in your lifetime you received your good things, while Lazarus received bad things, but now he is comforted here and you are in agony. And besides all this, between us and you a great chasm has been set in place, so that those who want to go from here to you cannot, nor can anyone cross over from there to us." He answered, "Then I beg you, father, send Lazarus to my family, for I have five brothers. Let him warn them, so that they will not also come to this place of torment." Abraham replied, "They have Moses and the Prophets; let them listen to them." "No, father Abraham," he said, "but if someone from the dead goes to them, they will repent." He said to him, "If they do not listen to Moses and the Prophets, they will not be convinced even if someone rises from the dead."

We see loudly and clearly the present condition in Hades. The rich man was alive, conscious, and in full exercise of his faculties; he had memory and was definitely in torment. When we consider that Jesus spoke on many subjects, He spoke twice as much on Hell

126

as He did on Heaven. Please be comforted like Lazarus was, by receiving God's grace through His Son, Jesus Christ. Believe in Jesus Christ for your only hope of salvation. Trust Him alone. Believe the Gospel, the very good news that Jesus died, He was buried, He rose from the dead, He was seen, He ascended into Heaven and, praise God, one day He will return—perhaps today! God has given each of us free will to choose. The choice is comfort or torment. Jesus proclaimed victoriously in Revelation 1:18, "I am the Living One; I was dead, and now look, I am alive for ever and ever! And I hold the keys of death and Hades." Death is the grave that claims the material part of man, the body. Hades is Hell that claims the immaterial part of man, the spirit. Jesus is the key to life.

Third, *Tartarus* is spoken of only one time in God's Word. It is found in 2 Peter 2:4 which reads, "For if God did not spare angels when they sinned, but sent them to hell, putting them in chains of darkness to be held for judgment." The word translated "hell" here is *Tartaros* in the Greek. It became our word Tartarus. I remember the name Tartarus by thinking of crème of tartar. It is the place where those angels whose special sin of leaving Heaven are confined. Let's emphasize that some of the wicked angels are bound in Tartarus and others are loosed on the earth. Those angels who are loosed we call evil spirits, wicked spirits, and demons under the command of Satan.

Jude 6 says, "And the angels who did not keep their positions of authority but abandoned their proper dwelling—these he has kept in darkness, bound with everlasting chains for judgment on the great Day." These angels did not keep their positions in Heaven. They abandoned Heaven, their own home! Some of the fallen angels were consigned or committed to Hell, to be incarcerated in prison. Tartarus is neither Hades nor Gehenna. It is the deepest abyss of Hades (Revelation 20:1-3; Isaiah 14:15). It is the pit. It is the subterranean abode of fallen angels, demonic hordes. Some fallen angels are bound in the abyss (Luke 8:31; Revelation 9:1-11). It is the depthless infernal bottomless pit. It is described as chains of darkness, pits of darkness, everlasting chains, and gloomy dungeons (2 Peter 2:1-9; Jude 1-7; 1 Corinthians 6:1-3).

They will be judged. Paul told the church at Corinth, "Do you not know that we will judge angels? How much more the things of this life" (1 Corinthians 6:3)! At the judgment of the sheep and the goats, this will be said, "Then he will say to those on his left, 'Depart from me, you who are cursed, into the eternal fire prepared for the devil and his angels'" (Matthew 25:41). Final Hell is prepared for the devil and the fallen angels. After Lucifer rebelled in Heaven, he took one-third of the angelic host with him in rebellion. "Its tail swept a third of the stars out of the sky and flung them to the earth" (Revelation 12:4). "The great dragon was hurled down—that ancient serpent called the devil, or Satan, who leads the whole world astray. He was hurled to the earth, and his angels with him" (Revelation 12:9). Read Luke 10:18, Ezekiel 28:11-19, Isaiah 14:12-21, and Revelation, chapter 12.

Fourth, the final main word where the wicked will be kept eternally, also a place of punishment, is Gehenna. It is the final abode of the unrighteous (Matthew 25:41). Gehenna has been prepared for the devil and his angels, but the wicked dead of all ages will share the same fate. What a grouping or coalition! The Beast, the False Prophet, Satan, and, after the Great White Throne Judgment, the lost of all ages will share the same fate: eternal separation from God, the second death. Gehenna is used twelve times in the New Testament. It is found once in the Book of James.

There was a garbage dump to the south and southwest of Jerusalem in the Valley of Hinnon or the Son of Hinnon. Fire and smoke spiraled constantly as carcasses of the sacrificial animals from the Temple worship were burned. It became a figure for Hell (2 Kings 23:10), symbolic of the final abode of the unrighteous. It is a place, not simply a state of mind (Revelation 20:14-15). It is for the embodied dead (Matthew 10:28; Luke 12:4-5), their final place forever and ever (Matthew 25:41). My son and I saw the Valley of Hinnon when we toured the Holy Land in 2000. It was a trip full of blessings! However, Gehenna will not be a blessing!

Who will be the first ones to be cast there? It will be the Beast and the False Prophet after the seven-year Tribulation (Revelation 19:19-21). Who will follow next? Satan will be hurled there (Revelation 20:10). Who will follow, finally? The lost of all ages will be cast there (Revelation 20:11-15). Gehenna is not a loss of being, but of well-being. There will be unmitigated judgment with no release, no letting up. It will never be softened or lessened (Isaiah 66:24). God answers the problem of evil in His justice and punishes sin. Extended descriptions of Gehenna are found in Matthew 5:28-30; 18:7-9; Mark 9:43-48.

"And they will go out and look on the dead bodies of those who rebelled against me; the worms that eat them will not die, the fire that burns them will not be quenched, and they will be loathsome to all mankind" (Isaiah 66:24). Here it signifies a worm that preys upon dead bodies. This is used metaphorically by the Lord. The statement in Isaiah 66:24 signifies the exclusion of hope of restoration because the punishment is eternal. Please accept Jesus Christ as your personal Lord and Savior. He will forgive you of your sins. He will give you life and peace. He will give you life, abundant life, here and forever.

The only time Gehenna is used outside the Gospels is by James. James is the half-brother of Jesus. "The tongue also is a fire, a world of evil among the parts of the body. It corrupts the whole body, sets the whole course of one's life on fire, and is itself set on fire by hell" (James 3:6). "Hell" here is Gehenna in the Greek. The tongue is spoken of in reference to Hell. The word stands for the powers of darkness whose characteristics and destiny are those of Hell. Hell here is described as the source of evil done by misuse of the tongue. We can *kill with the tongue*. Words can kill. "With the tongue we praise our Lord and Father, and with it we curse human beings, who have been made in God's likeness. Out of the same mouth come praise and cursing. My brothers and sisters, this should not be" (James 3:9-10).

The Great White Throne Judgment is real. It is the final judgment day. Jesus will judge the works of mankind, all who are outside His saving grace. He died on Calvary so this would not have to happen. Paul says to the church at Rome,

> But now apart from the law the righteousness of God has been made known, to which the law and the Prophets testify. This righteousness is given through faith in Jesus Christ to all who believe. There is no difference between Jew and Gentile, for all have sinned and fall short of the

> glory of God, and all are justified freely by his grace
> through the redemption that came by Christ Jesus. God
> presented Christ as a sacrifice of atonement through the
> shedding of his blood—to be received by faith. He did this
> to demonstrate his righteousness, because in his forbear-
> ance he had left the sins committed beforehand unpun-
> ished—he did it to demonstrate his righteousness at the
> present time, so as to be just and the one who justifies
> those who have faith in Jesus. (Romans 3:21-26)

God is just. God is the justifier of the one who has faith in Jesus Christ. The Judge of all the earth will do right. Abraham spoke of God's judgment, "Far be it from you to do such a thing—to kill the righteous with the wicked, treating the righteous and the wicked alike. Far be it from you! Will not the Judge of all the earth do right" (Genesis 18:25)? Jesus will act justly at the Great White Throne Judgment. The wicked are sent to their doom. They have not exercised faith in Jesus. The next and final chapter will take us past the Great White Throne Judgment into the great timeless forever.

Note: A great resource on the subject matter of this chapter is the work by Dwight Pentecost, *Things to Come*.

EIGHT

The Great Timeless Forever

By the same word the present heavens and earth are reserved for fire, being kept for the day of judgment and destruction of the ungodly. But do not forget this one thing, dear friends: With the Lord a day is like a thousand years, and a thousand years are like a day. The Lord is not slow in keeping his promise, as some understand slowness. Instead he is patient with you, not wanting anyone to perish, but everyone to come to repentance. But the day of the Lord will come like a thief. The heavens will disappear with a roar; the elements will be destroyed by fire, and the earth and everything done in it will be laid bare. Since everything will be destroyed in this way, what kind of people ought you to be? You ought to live holy and godly lives as you look forward to the day of God and speed its coming. That day will bring about the destruction of the heavens by fire, and the elements will melt in the heat. But in keeping with his promise we are looking forward to a new heaven and a new earth, where righteousness dwells. (2 Peter 3:7-13)

"'As the new heavens and the new earth that I make will endure before me,' declares the LORD, 'so will your name and descendants endure.'" (Isaiah 66:22)

The great timeless forever is the eternal state (Revelation 21 and 22). The eternal state is one of no end, with blessing for the redeemed and remorse for the lost. God will create New Heavens and a New Earth and the eternal state begins where God provides a place for the redeemed of all ages in the heavenly city of Jerusalem, the New Jerusalem, our eternal home. Today, we are looking forward to God creating all things new. We have already seen what happens to the old Heavens and earth. They will be purged by God. God has revealed His promise: "But in keeping with his promise we are looking forward to a new heaven and a new earth, where righteousness dwells" (2 Peter 3:13). It will be an eternal home of righteousness. Isaiah prophesied, "See, I will create new heavens and a new earth. The former things will not be remembered, nor will they come to mind" (Isaiah 65:17). Isaiah continued in chapter 66, verse 22: "'As the new heavens and the new earth that I make will endure before me,' declares the LORD, 'so will your name and descendants endure.'" God will create the new heavens and the new earth after the Great White Throne Judgment, and they will be eternal. I love it that God reveals "the former things will not be remembered, nor will they come to mind."

Personally, I don't want to be reminded for eternity of my sinful nature. For the believer, in eternity our sinful nature won't even be brought to mind. However, those who stand at the Great White Throne Judgment will be reminded for eternity that their wages for sin led to death, the second death, which is eternal separation from God. The Apostle Paul said it this way, "For the wages of sin is death, but the gift of God is eternal life in Christ Jesus our Lord" (Romans 6:23). I don't want to be eternally separated from God or His presence! Believers are not judged at the Great White Throne Judgment; we are judged at The Great Testing at the Judgment Seat (Bema) of Christ. What has been revealed will be my works after I was saved. I will find out if my works after I was saved qualified for a reward or not. Then the Church of Jesus Christ will be married to Christ and, from that point on, former things will be forgotten and we will not have them brought to our attention again.

"Then I saw 'a new heaven and a new earth,' for the first heaven and the first earth had passed away, and there was no longer any sea" (Revelation 21:1). The Apostle John witnessed the future creation of God, after the purging of creation. We have covered the four specific events that must take place between the closing of the Millennium and the eternal state (the great timeless forever): the release and revolt of Satan, the purging of creation, the judgment of the final impenitent (the Great White Throne Judgment), and creation of the New Heavens and New Earth. It's wonderful to think about John 14:1-7. It reads,

> Do not let your hearts be troubled. You believe in God; believe also in me. My Father's house has many rooms; if that were not so, would I have told you that I am going there to prepare a place for you? And if I go and prepare a place for you, I will come back and take you to be with me that you also may be where I am. You know the way to the place where I am going. Thomas said to him, "Lord, we don't know where you are going, so how can we know the way?" Jesus answered, "I am the way and the truth and the life. No one comes to the Father except through me. If you really know me, you will know my Father as well. From now on, you do know him and have seen him."

Jesus has gone to prepare a place for us. His Father's house has many dwelling places, rooms, mansions; room for all who believe. I believe the place Jesus is preparing for us is the New Jerusalem, the Heavenly City.

The New Heavens and the New Earth await us. Several Greek words are used for *new*. The Greek word new in 2 Peter 3:13 is *kainos*. The meaning is not new in time. It means that which is not recent, but new in freshness. It is new as to form or quality. If God were going to let it be recent or new in respect of time and age, the Greek word for new, **neos**, would have been used. God is not going to make a new set of Heavens and earth. God is going to purge the old Heavens and earth and from those ashes create the New Heavens and New Earth. They will be changed and purged with fire. Peter uses the word *kainos* in 2 Peter 3:10-13. The word new here suggests fresh life that rises from the decay and wreck of the old Heavens and

133

old earth. Our eternal home is the home of righteousness. God's people can speed the Day of Christ by prayer, living a sanctified life, accomplishing God's purposes, and evangelism.

I am an optimist. Jesus is coming at the Rapture *for* us. Jesus is coming at the Revelation *with* us. Revelation 22:20 says, "He who testifies to these things says, 'Yes, I am coming soon.' 'Amen. Come, Lord Jesus.'" The response of John here and my response also is *Amen! Come, Lord Jesus!* I pray it is your response, too.

What is the description of the New Jerusalem? It is found in these verses:

One of the seven angels who had the seven bowls full of the seven last plagues came and said to me, "Come, I will show you the bride, the wife of the Lamb." And he carried me away in the Spirit to a mountain great and high, and showed me the Holy City, Jerusalem, coming down out of heaven from God. It shone with the glory of God, and its brilliance was like that of a very precious jewel, like a jasper, clear as crystal. It had a great, high wall with twelve gates, and with twelve angels at the gates. On the gates were written the names of the twelve tribes of Israel. There were three gates on the east, three on the north, three on the south and three on the west. The wall of the city had twelve foundations, and on them were the names of the twelve apostles of the Lamb. The angel who talked with me had a measuring rod of gold to measure the city, its gates and its walls. The city was laid out like a square, as long as it was wide. He measured the city with the rod and found it to be 12,000 stadia in length, and as wide and high as it is long. The angel measured the wall using human measurement, and it was 144 cubits thick. The wall was made of jasper, and the city of pure gold, as pure as glass. The foundations of the city walls were deco-rated with every kind of precious stone. The first founda-tion was jasper, the second sapphire, the third agate, the fourth emerald, the fifth onyx, the sixth ruby, the seventh chrysolite, the eighth beryl, the ninth topaz, the tenth turquoise, the eleventh jacinth, and the twelfth amethyst. The twelve gates were twelve pearls, each gate made of a single pearl. The great street of the city was of gold, as pure as transparent glass. I did not see a temple in the city, because the Lord God Almighty and the Lamb are its temple. The city does not need the sun or the moon to shine on it, for the glory of God gives it light, and the Lamb is its lamp." (Revelation 21:9-23)

The New Jerusalem is a glorious, well-protected, accessible, well-founded, beautiful, templeless city, and it is divinely illuminated.

How is the city constructed? It has a great, high wall. There are twelve gates of pearls, glistening in appearance. It is also a very accessible city with twelve gates. The names of the twelve tribes of Israel are inscribed on the gates; three gates in each direction. Angels are also stationed at the gates. The wall and the gates suggest that security of the Bride (Revelation 21:9; 21:12).

Next, twelve foundations with the names of the twelve apostles of the Lamb inscribed on them are revealed. The twelve tribes of Israel and the twelve Apostles of the Lamb, Jesus Christ, are all in the eternal state. They are distinguished, but all are included in God's redemption program.

God will construct this city. The author of Hebrews tells us clearly,

For he (Abraham) was looking forward to the city with foundations, whose architect and builder is God. And by faith even Sarah, who was past childbearing age, was enabled to bear children because she considered him faithful who had made the promise. And so from this one man, and he as good as dead, came descendants as numerous as the stars in the sky and as countless as the sand on the seashore. All these people were still living by faith when they died. They did not receive the things promised; they only saw them and welcomed them from a distance, admitting that they were foreigners and strangers on earth. People who say such things show that

> they are looking for a country of their own. If they had
> been thinking of the country they had left, they would
> have had opportunity to return. Instead, they were longing
> for a better country—a heavenly one. Therefore God is
> not ashamed to be called their God, for he has prepared
> a city for them. (Hebrews 11:10-16)

The sole architect and builder is God. "In the beginning was the Word, and the Word was with God, and the Word was God. He was with God in the beginning. Through him all things were made; without him nothing was made that has been made" (John 1:1-2). Through Jesus Christ all things were made. All things past, present, and future exist because of Jesus Christ.

What is the measurement of the city? An angel measures the New Jerusalem, along with its gates and walls, with a rod of gold. The New Jerusalem is foursquare. The angel measures the length, width, and height, each 12,000 stadia (approximately 1,380 miles), forming a perfect foursquare designed by God. Foursquare is seen several times in the Old Testament. The altar of burnt offering and the altar of incense (Exodus 27:1; 30:1-2) in the Tabernacle and later the Temple were foursquare. The High Priest wore a breastplate (Exodus 28:15-16) foursquare; it was nine inches by nine inches. In Solomon's Temple, the Holy of Holies (2 Chronicles 3:1-13; 1 Kings 6:20), was laid out foursquare. It was thirty feet by thirty feet. Ezekiel's prophecy of a new city and temple is foursquare (Ezekiel 41:21; 43:16; 45:1; 48:20).

The wall is 144 cubits, or 216 feet, thick. The wall is made of jasper (green quartz). The foundations are decorated or adorned with every kind of precious stone or gem. "The twelve gates were twelve pearls, each gate made of a single pearl. The great street of the city was of gold, as pure as transparent glass" (Revelation 21:21). Precious stones, gold, and pearls—*oh my!* Trying to take it all in and comprehend the majesty of the New Jerusalem is hard to do. However, from this picture of the New Jerusalem, it is a lovely place, but the beauty cannot compare to our Savior, Jesus Christ, who is altogether lovely (Song of Songs 5:16)!

The New Jerusalem is holy, with no need of a temple and no need of our sun and moon. John says this in Revelation 21:22-27. John continues in Revelation 22:3-5: "No longer will there be any curse. The throne of God and of the Lamb will be in the city, and his servants will serve him. They will see his face, and his name will be on their foreheads. There will be no more night. They will not need the light of a lamp or the light of the sun, for the Lord God will give them light. And they will reign for ever and ever." Jesus is Light. "When Jesus spoke again to the people, he said, 'I am the light of the world. Whoever follows me will never walk in darkness, but will have the light of life'" (John 8:12). Jesus is the Temple. Jesus told the Jews, 'Destroy this temple, and I will raise it again in three days'" (John 2:19).

I love the picture of the inhabitants of the New Jerusalem. The author of Hebrews pictures it so wonderfully for us to comprehend.

> But you have come to Mount Zion, to the city of the living God, the heavenly Jerusalem. You have come to thousands upon thousands of angels in joyful assembly, to the church of the firstborn, whose names are written in heaven. You have come to God, the Judge of all, to the spirits of the righteous made perfect, to Jesus the mediator of a new covenant, and to the sprinkled blood that speaks a better word than the blood of Abel. (Hebrews 12:22-24)

In this great City, God is there. Angels are there. The Church of the firstborn is there. Our names are written in *Heaven!* The saints from all ages, even those outside of the Church Age, are there. Jesus, our Mediator, is there with His blood sprinkled before God on the mercy seat of Heaven. By faith today, we have come to Mount Zion. I believe the city is the city of the living God, the Heavenly Jerusalem, the New Jerusalem. What a place and how blessed are the redeemed who are with God for eternity. You talk about the eternal state, the great timeless forever. Well, here it is!

Revelation 22 reveals the river of life and the tree of life.

> On the last and greatest day of the festival (The Feast of Tabernacles), Jesus stood and said in a loud voice, "Let anyone who is thirsty come to me and drink. Whoever believes in me, as Scripture has said, rivers of living water will flow from within them." By this he meant the Spirit, whom those who believed in him were later to receive. Up to that time the Spirit had not been given, since Jesus had not yet been glorified. (John 7:37-39)

Both the river of life and the tree of life stand for our abundant spiritual life with God for all eternity. the tree of life is reminiscent of God's creation in Genesis 2:8-9 and 2:15-17. God has always given us the free will to choose life. Adam chose differently. His sin brought penalty, guilt, and shame to himself, Eve, and all their descendants, down to you and me. I've chosen life in Jesus Christ. Are you Rapture ready?

Hear Jesus now: "Look, I am coming soon! Blessed is the one who keeps the words of the prophecy written in this scroll" (Revelation 22:7). "Look, I am coming soon! My reward is with me, and I will give to each person according to what they have done" (Revelation 22:12). "He who testifies to these things says, 'Yes, I am coming soon.' 'Amen. Come, Lord Jesus'" (Revelation 22:20). We are saved in His name alone. We eagerly wait for His Coming.

The Apostle Paul knew his time to die was at hand. Some of his last words written were these,

> In the presence of God and of Christ Jesus, who will judge the living and the dead, and in view of his appearing and his kingdom, I give you this charge: Preach the word; be prepared in season and out of season; correct, rebuke and encourage—with great patience and careful instruction. For the time will come when people will not put up with sound doctrine. Instead, to suit their own desires, they will gather around them a great number of teachers to say what their itching ears want to hear. They will turn their ears away from the truth and turn aside to myths. But you, keep your head in all situations, endure hardship,

> do the work of an evangelist, discharge all the duties of your ministry. For I am already being poured out like a drink offering, and the time for my departure is near. I have fought the good fight, I have finished the race, I have kept the faith. Now there is in store for me the crown of righteousness, which the Lord, the righteous Judge, will award to me on that day—and not only to me, but also to all who have longed for his appearing. (2 Timothy 4:1-8)

"Longed" in the Greek is *agapao*. It is Divine love. It is a constant, steadfast, enduring, and covenant love. It is love that seeks the highest good in another person. It is love that gives freely without expecting love in return. Love is all this and much more (1 Corinthians 13). It is the greatest gift. I love Christ's appearing. I am Rapture ready, ready for the great trumpeting translation. I pray our generation is the Rapture generation. However, until the time Christ returns, we are to serve Him by ministering to others. We are to pray for the lost, seek their salvation, serve the Body of Christ, and share the good news. Christ died for our sins. He was placed in a borrowed tomb. He rose from the dead on the third day. After forty days on earth He ascended into Heaven. He is at the Father's right hand interceding for us. He is our Advocate. So, one day, perhaps today, He is coming at the Rapture. Then, the prophetic clock will tick again for God's chosen people, the nation of Israel. Seven years will pass with great trouble, the Great Tribulation. During this time, we will stand at the Bema seat of Christ, judged for our works after salvation, the great testing. We will come back with Christ at the great triumph. He will set up His Kingdom on earth at the Millennium, the great ten centuries. After the one thousand years, He will judge the lost of all ages at the Great White Throne Judgment. After that, eternity will begin, the great timeless forever.

Indeed, these are seven great and true future events. Blessings! And, I am praying you are Rapture ready!

Note: A great resource on the subject matter of this chapter is the work by Charles Caldwell Ryrie, *Revelation*.

Appendix A

The Bible—Man's Authority

In past years, you may remember singing with hymns, spiritual songs, and praise choruses about the wonders of the Bible, God's Word. "The B-I-B-L-E, yes that's the Book for me. I stand alone on the Word of God, the B-I-B-L-E." How do you demonstrate your commitment to the authority of God's Word?

To come to the realization that the Bible, God's special revelation to man, is the absolute authority in your life, faith, and practice, a change in mind and heart must occur. To be born again means we have come to God by faith alone trusting that His Word that reveals how to be saved and go to Heaven is true. It is the only way to Heaven.

You must choose to have God's authority and sovereign control over your life. Until that decision is sealed, your flesh (sin nature) is in control of your life. Your life is under the authority of its dictates, resulting in confusion, wrong decisions, and wayward actions.

If you are under the authority of God's Word, then the Holy Spirit witnesses with your spirit that you are a child of God. The Holy Spirit guides you into all truth. Jesus said in John 17:17, "Sanctify them by the truth; your word is truth." You cannot separate the Holy Spirit of God from truth. Experience, reason, or any other authority does not determine truth. Truth is determined only through the Scriptures. The Word of God and the Holy Spirit must be united in truth. Truth lies deeper than the theological statement of it. You must be Spirit-taught. Then, and only then, are you truly under the authority of God's Word in your life.

You realize as you yield yourself to the teaching of God's Word that, in all matters, it gives instruction and is absolutely authoritative. Listen to Paul explaining to Timothy this wonderful truth, "All Scripture is God-breathed and is useful for teaching, rebuking, correcting and training in righteousness, so that the servant of God may be thoroughly equipped for every good work" (2 Timothy 3:16-17). The authority comes from the writings being God-breathed. It is the inbreathing by God of life in His Word. The Bible is the product of the creative breath of God.

Aren't you glad you are no longer under your authority, but under God's authority, the Bible?

Rev. Terry Burnside

This article was written in 2006 when Central Church in Collierville, Tennessee studied the *40 Days of Faith: Discovering the Uniqueness of Christianity*, written by the leadership of Central Church, both Elders and the Senior Team. There were forty articles. I had the privilege of writing three of these articles.

Appendix B

The following outline and Scriptures warrant your personal study:

I. Definition of Prophecy

A. Prophecy is the Divine revelation of future events.

Isaiah 46:10: "I make known the end from the beginning, from ancient times, what is still to come. I say, 'My purpose will stand, and I will do all that I please.'"

2 Peter 1:19-21: "We also have the prophetic message as something completely reliable, and you will do well to pay attention to it, as to a light shining in a dark place, until the day dawns and the morning star rises in your hearts. Above all, you must understand that no prophecy of Scripture came about by the prophet's own interpretation of things. For prophecy never had its origin in the human will, but prophets, though human, spoke from God as they were carried along by the Holy Spirit."

B. Prophecy is the light shining in a dark place.

2 Peter 1:19: "We also have the prophetic message as something completely reliable, and you will do well to pay attention to it, as to a light shining in a dark place, until the day dawns and the morning star rises in your hearts."

C. Prophecy is God's history written in advance.

Isaiah 46:10: "I make known the end from the beginning, from ancient times, what is still to come. I say, 'My purpose will stand, and I will do all that I please.'"

II. The Intention of Prophecy

A. Prophetic study is intended to lead to a deeper spiritual life. It leads you into deeper spiritual things (truths).

B. Prophetic study is intended to be a blessing and a source of encouragement.

III. The Prophet of God who Spoke Prophecy

A. A prophet was God's spokesman, His mouthpiece. He spoke for God. The prophet of God, who spoke prophecy, accurately wrote down what God wanted us to know. My life has been changed because of God's Word, especially prophecy.

B. What was the acid test of a true prophet? The Bible is very clear on what the acid test of a true prophet is: what he spoke came true!

Deuteronomy 18:15-22: "The LORD your God will raise up for you a prophet like me from among you, from your fellow Israelites. You must listen to him. For this is what you asked of the LORD your God at Horeb on the day of the assembly when you said, 'Let us not hear the voice of the LORD our God nor see this great fire anymore, or we will die.' The LORD said to me: 'What they say is good. I will raise up for them a prophet like you from among their fellow Israelites, and I will put my words in his mouth. He will tell them everything I command him. I myself will call to account anyone who does not listen to my words that the prophet speaks in my name. But a prophet who presumes to speak in my name anything I have not commanded, or a prophet who speaks in the name of other gods, is to be put to death. You may say to yourselves, 'How can we know when a message has not been spoken by the LORD?' If what a prophet proclaims in the name of the LORD does not take place or come true, that is a message the LORD has not spoken. That prophet has spoken presumptuously, so do not be alarmed.'"

It is recorded in the Book of Acts that some prophets came from Jerusalem to Antioch. One of the prophets was Agabus. He stood in front of the believers and, through the Holy Spirit, made a prediction that the entire Roman world would experience a severe famine. The famine took place during the reign of Claudius. The believers took action by providing help for their fellow brothers living in Judea. We read in Acts 11:27-30: "During this time some prophets came down from Jerusalem to Antioch. One of them, named Agabus, stood up and through the Spirit predicted that a severe famine would spread over the entire Roman world. (This happened during the reign of Claudius.) The disciples, as each one was able, decided to provide help for the brothers and sisters living in Judea. This they did, sending their gift to the elders by Barnabas and Saul." Agabus was a true prophet. What he prophesied happened.

Later, Agabus prophesied again, "Coming over to us, he took Paul's belt, tied his own hands and feet with it and said, 'The Holy Spirit says, In this way the Jewish leaders in Jerusalem will bind the owner of this belt and will hand him over to the Gentiles'" (Acts 21:11). Verse 33 of Acts 21 says, "The commander came up and arrested him and ordered him to be bound with two chains. Then he asked who he was and what he had done." The Apostle Paul was arrested. Paul was bound with chains. Paul was handed over to the Gentiles. What Agabus prophesied came true. Again, the acid test of a true prophet was that what he had prophesied came to pass.

IV. Prophecy is Both Fulfilled and Predictive

Many prophecies have already been fulfilled; the rest are still waiting to be fulfilled, being predictive prophecy.

Twenty-seven percent of the Bible deals with prophecy!

One out of every twelve verses in the New Testament deals with the Second Coming! In the epistles, the Second Coming is found in one out of ten verses!

On the day that Jesus Christ died for our sins on the Cross of Calvary, thirty-three prophecies were fulfilled. You will find the list of the prophecies fulfilled in one day, in Appendix C "Thirty-three Prophecies Fulfilled in One Day." For one prophecy to come to pass on one particular day is amazing in itself, but to have thirty-three prophecies fulfilled in just one day is overwhelming proof that God's Word is His promise, oath, and fulfillment. Read Luke 24. This chapter speaks of the resurrection of Jesus Christ. On that day, two from Jerusalem were traveling back to their village called Emmaus, about seven miles from Jerusalem. We have the name of one traveler, Cleopas. They were in deep conversation about all that had happened concerning Jesus over the last few days in Jerusalem. Jesus approached them and joined the conversation. Their eyes were restrained, so they did not know it was Jesus speaking with them. The two spoke of Jesus of Nazareth, the mighty Prophet in word and deed, His betrayal, and His condemnation to die by crucifixion. They were hoping that He was the one to redeem Israel. Before they left Jerusalem, they heard the report that Jesus was alive. Jesus then spoke to them. "He said to them, 'How foolish you are, and how slow to believe all that the prophets have spoken! Did not the

146

Messiah have to suffer these things and then enter his glory'" (Luke 24:25-26)? After saying this, Jesus explained all the Scriptures that referred to Him. Later that day, Jesus appeared to His disciples, the eleven and those who were with them. In the conversation that followed, He shared many things. Luke 24:44-48 are some of the most illuminating words of Scripture concerning prophecy, both fulfilled and predictive.

> He said to them, "This is what I told you while I was still with you: Everything must be fulfilled that is written about me in the law of Moses, the Prophets and the Psalms." Then he opened their minds so they could understand the Scriptures. He told them, "This is what is written: The Messiah will suffer and rise from the dead on the third day, and repentance for the forgiveness of sins will be preached in his name to all nations, beginning at Jerusalem. You are witnesses of these things." (Luke 24:44-48)

Jesus wants us to understand the Scriptures. Indeed, you can prick any verse in God's Word and it will bleed the blood of Jesus Christ. Jesus is the *Logos*, the Living Word. All God's written Word points to Him. To God be the glory!

V. Prophecy and Eschatology

Relationship: Eschatology is a division of prophecy. Eschatology is the study of future, final, and last things dealing with events beyond this present life (beyond death) and this present age (Church Age).

VI. Three Strange Prophecies of the Old Testament

A. Joshua's prophecy concerning Jericho:
   Joshua 6:26, 27; 1 Kings 16:29-34

Joshua gave this prophecy in 1400 B.C., and it was fulfilled in 874 B.C., exactly 526 years later. We started this book with this solemn warning from Joshua. Joshua's words came to pass. It was fulfilled literally. Literalness is important to understand all prophecies.

B. The man of God from Judah's prophecy concerning the altar:
1 Kings 13:1-34; 2 Kings 23:15-30

The man of God from Judah gave this prophecy in 931 B.C., and it was fulfilled in 622 B.C., exactly 309 years later. In 931 B.C., the Kingdom of Israel was divided. Upon division, the Northern Kingdom, called Israel, comprised ten tribes. Jeroboam, the son of Nebat, was the first King. The Southern Kingdom, called Judah, comprised only two tribes, Judah and Benjamin. Rehoboam, the son of Solomon, was the first king of Judah. The nation had been unified under Saul, David, and Solomon for one hundred twenty years. Each reign was forty years for these three kings. However, after the death of Solomon, the Kingdom was divided.

C. Elisha's prophecy concerning the Moabites:
2 Kings 3:14-27

Elisha's prophecy was in 852 B.C. It was fulfilled in less than 24 hours.

VII. Application: *God's Word Always Comes to Fulfillment!*
1 Kings 8:56; 2 Corinthians 1:20

Appendix C

"33 Prophecies Fulfilled in One Day"

1. Prophecy—The betrayal of the Lord Jesus Christ by Judas, 1,000 B.C.
Psalm 41:9; 2 Samuel 23:1-7. David is the "Sweet Psalmist of Israel."
Fulfillment: John 13:2, 18-19; 6:70-71; Mark 14:10-11; Acts 1:15-20.

2. Prophecy—It was predicted that the Lord Jesus Christ would be forsaken by His disciples 500 years before it took place. Zechariah 13:7.
Fulfillment: Matthew 26:31-32; Mark 14:48-52.

3. Prophecy—The price paid for His betrayal was foretold. Zechariah 11:12.
Fulfillment: Matthew 26:14-16; Exodus 21:32.

4. Prophecy—What would be done with the money? How Judas would use the betrayal money. Zechariah 11:13.
Fulfillment: Matthew 27:1-10; Jeremiah 19:1-13; 18:2-12; Jeremiah 32:6-9.

5. Prophecy—His scourging. Isaiah 50:6.
Fulfillment: Matthew 26:67-68; 27:26-30; John 10:17-18; Deuteronomy 25:3.

6. Prophecy—Shame, reproach, dishonor, mocking, discredit, disgrace, and scorn. Psalm 69:19-21.
Fulfillment: Matthew 27:26-31; Hebrews 12:2; Galatians 3:13; Deuteronomy 21:22-23; Hebrews 13:12-13.

7. Prophecy—False witnesses against Christ at His trial. Psalm 35:11-12.
Fulfillment: Mark 14:55-65.

8. Prophecy—The Smitten Shepherd. Zechariah 13:7.
Fulfillment: Matthew 26:31.

9. Prophecy—The parting of His garments. Psalm 22:18.
Fulfillment: John 19:23-24.

10. Prophecy—The Lord Jesus Christ would not open His mouth at His trial. Isaiah 53:7.
Fulfillment: Matthew 27:11-14; Luke 23:1-12.

11. Prophecy—Our Savior's crucifixion. Isaiah 53:4-10.
Fulfillment: Luke 23:33; Matthew 27:33; Mark 15:22; John 19:17.

12. Prophecy—He would fall beneath the Cross. Psalm 109:24-25.
Fulfillment: John 19:16-17; Matthew 27:32; Luke 23:26, 27; 22:24-44; 24:25-48.

13. Prophecy—His thirst. Psalm 69:3, 21; Psalm 22:15.
Fulfillment: John 19:28.

14. Prophecy—What would they give Him to drink? Psalm 69:21.
Fulfillment: Matthew 27:34; John 19:29-30.

15. Prophecy—They stared at Jesus on the Cross. Psalm 22:13-17.
Fulfillment: Matthew 27:36; Luke 23:48-49.

16. Prophecy—The pierced hands and feet. Psalm 22:16.
Fulfillment: Matthew 27:35; Romans 3:24; Acts 4:12.

Consider as you meditate on these verses: Was the atonement necessary? Could God redeem man some other way than the Cross?

17. Prophecy—The pierced side. Zechariah 12:10; 13:6.
Fulfillment: Luke 23:35; John 19:31-37; Revelation 1:7; 1 Peter 1:2, 18-19; Ephesians 5:26.

18. Prophecy—His heart was broken. Psalm 22:14.
Fulfillment: John 19:34.

19. Prophecy—Our Lord's mother and friends. Psalm 38:11.
Fulfillment: Luke 23:48-49; John 19:25-27; Luke 2:21-40.

20. Prophecy—Mockery of the people. Psalm 109:24-25.
Fulfillment: Matthew 27:39-40.

21. Prophecy—Railing, hatred, and taunting by the mob. Psalm 22:6-8.
Fulfillment: Matthew 27:41-44; 1 Peter 2:23-25; John 15:22-25; Psalm 35:19; 69:3-4; 109:1-5.

22. Prophecy—The Lamb of God. Isaiah 53:7.
Fulfillment: John 1:29-36; Hebrews 2:9; 1 John 2:2; John 3:16; Ephesians 5:25; Galatians 2:20.

23. Prophecy—His intercession for the transgressors. Isaiah 53:12.
Fulfillment: Luke 23:34; Ephesians 2:18; Matthew 26:47-56.

24. Prophecy—The intense lonely cry in the midnight hour of His suffering. Psalm 22:1.
Fulfillment: Matthew 27:46.

25. Prophecy—His marred visage, due to the brutality of the soldiers. Isaiah 52:14.
Fulfillment: John 19:5, 14; John 12:22-25.

26. Prophecy—Cry of victory and triumph. Psalm 22:31.
Fulfillment: John 19:30.

27. Prophecy—The Lord Jesus Christ commends His Spirit to His Father. Psalm 31:5.
Fulfillment: Luke 23:46; Hebrews 9:27; James 2:26.

28. Prophecy—A wonderful prophecy uttered 1,490 years before its fulfillment. Exodus 12:46; Psalm 34:20.
Fulfillment: John 19:33-36.

29. Prophecy—It was foretold 700 years before that He was to be numbered with the transgressors. Isaiah 53:12.
Fulfillment: Luke 23:33.

30. Prophecy—The Messiah was to be cut off, but not for Himself. Daniel 9:26.
Fulfillment: John 11:50-52.

31. Prophecy—The oldest prophecy of all, uttered by the Lord Himself, at least 4,000 years before... Genesis 3:15.
Fulfillment: John 19:18; 12:31-33; Romans 16:20.

32. Prophecy—The place of the burial of the body of the Lord Jesus Christ is predicted. Isaiah 53:9.
Fulfillment: Matthew 27:57-60.

33. Prophecy—A great Calvary miracle prophecy; wonderful and uttered about 800 years before it was fulfilled. Amos 8:9.
Fulfillment: Matthew 27:45.

I acknowledge the arrangement of these thirty-three prophecies by Rev. Charles G. Bauer. He provided some of the Scriptures listed. Over the years, I have added more Scripture passages to each specific prophecy and the fulfillment.

Chosen People Ministries, Inc., lists twenty-seven of the thirty-three prophecies I have included. Used by permission.

APPENDIX D

Behold, the Bridegroom Comes!

Renald E. Showers

The Comforting Promise

It was a night of destiny. Jesus had gathered with His disciples in the Upper Room. In a few more hours He would be crucified on a cross. Jesus had been warning His disciples concerning His coming death, resurrection, and ascension to Heaven. The prospect of these events caused the disciples to be greatly disturbed. To ease their fears, Jesus made the following comforting promise:

Let not your heart be troubled; ye believe in God, believe also in me. In my Father's house are many mansions: if it were not so, I would have told you. I go to prepare a place for you. And if I go and prepare a place for you, I will come again, and receive you unto myself; that where I am, there ye may be also (John. 14:1-3).

Jewish Marriage Customs

Those who live in the modern western world do not catch the full significance of Jesus' promise. This is because Jesus was drawing an analogy from Jewish marriage customs in biblical times. We must examine those marriage customs if we want to grasp the significance of His promise.

The first major step in a Jewish marriage was betrothal. Betrothal involved the establishment of a marriage covenant. By Jesus' time, this covenant was usually established as the result of the prospective bridegroom taking the initiative. The prospective bridegroom would travel from his father's house to the home of the prospective bride. There he negotiated with the young woman's father to determine the price (*mohar*) he must pay to purchase his bride. When the bridegroom paid the purchase price, the marriage covenant was established; and the young man and woman were regarded as husband and wife. From that moment on, the bride was declared to be consecrated or sanctified—set apart exclusively for her bridegroom. As a symbol of the covenant relationship that had been established, the man and his bride drank from a cup of wine over which a betrothal benediction had been pronounced.

After the marriage covenant had been established, the bridegroom left the bride's home and returned to his father's house. There he would remain separated from his bride for twelve months. This period of separation gave the bride time to gather her trousseau and prepare for married life. Meanwhile, the bridegroom prepared living accommodations in his father's house to which he could bring his bride.

At the end of the separation, the man came to take his bride to live with him. The taking of the bride usually occurred at night. The bridegroom, best man, and other male escorts would leave the bridegroom's father's house and conduct a torch light procession to the bride's home. Although the bride was expecting her bridegroom to come for her, she did not know exactly when he would arrive. As a result, the bridegroom's arrival would be preceded by a shout. This shout forewarned the bride to be prepared for the coming of the bridegroom.

After the bridegroom received his bride and her female attendants, the enlarged wedding party returns from the bride's home to the bridegroom's father's house. Upon arrival there, the wedding party would find that the wedding guests had assembled already.

Shortly after the bride and bridegroom arrived, the other members would escort them to the bridal chamber (*huppah*). Before entering the chamber the bride remained veiled so that no one could see her face. While the groomsmen and bridesmaids would wait outside, the bride and bridegroom would enter the bridal chamber alone. There, in private, the couple entered a physical union for the first time, thereby consummating the marriage that had been covenanted earlier.

After the marriage was consummated, the bridegroom would announce the consummation to the other members of the wedding party waiting outside the chamber (John 3:29). These people relayed the news of the marital union to the wedding guests. After receiving the good news, the wedding guests feast and make merry for the next seven days.

During the seven days of the wedding festivities, which were sometimes called "the seven days of the *huppah*," the bride remained hidden in the bridal chamber. At the end of these seven days, the bridegroom brought his bride out of the bridal chamber, now with her veil removed, so all could see who his bride was.

The Examination of the Analogy

Now that we have considered the marriage, we can examine the analogy Jesus drew in John 14. In what ways was Jesus' promise analogous with Jewish marriage customs?

First, we can note that the Scriptures regard the church to be the Bride of Christ (Ephesians 5:22-23). Just as the Jewish bridegroom took the initiative in marriage by leaving his father's house and traveling to the prospective bride's home, so Jesus left His Father's house in heaven more than 2,000 years ago and traveled to earth, the home of His prospective church.

In the same manner as the Jewish bridegroom came to the bride's home to obtain her through the establishing a marriage covenant, so Jesus came to earth to obtain the church through the establishment of a covenant. On the same night Jesus made His promise in John 14, He instituted Communion. As He passed the cup of wine to His disciples, He said, "This cup is the new testament (covenant) in my blood" (1 Corinthians 11:25). This was His way of saying that He would establish a new covenant through the shedding of His blood on the cross.

Parallel to the custom of the Jewish bridegroom paying a price to purchase his bride, Jesus paid a price to purchase His bride, the church. The price He paid was His own life blood. Because of this purchase price, Paul wrote the following to members of the church: "Know ye not that...ye are not your own? For ye are bought with a price: therefore, glorify God in your body" (1 Corinthians 6:19-20).

Analogous with the Jewish bride being sanctified or set apart exclusively for her bridegroom after the marriage covenant was established, the church has been declared to be sanctified or set apart exclusively for Christ (Ephesians 5:25-27; 1 Corinthians 1:2; 6:11; Hebrews 10:10; 13:12).

In the same way that a cup of wine served as a symbol of the marriage covenant through which the Jewish bridegroom obtained his bride, so the cup of Communion serves as the symbol of the covenant through which Christ has obtained the church (1 Corinthians 11:25).

Just as the Jewish bridegroom left his bride's home and returned to his father's house after the marriage covenant had been established, so Jesus left the earth, the home of the church, and returned to His Father's house in heaven after He had established the new covenant and risen from the dead (John 6:62; 20:17).

In correspondence with the period of separation between the Jewish bridegroom and bride, Christ has remained separate from the church for over 2000 years. The church is now living in that period of separation.

Parallel to the custom of the Jewish bridegroom preparing living accommodations for his bride in his father's house during the time of separation, Christ has been preparing living accommodations for the church in His Father's house in heaven during His separation from His Bride (John 14:2).

In the same manner as the Jewish bridegroom came to take his bride to live with him at the end of the separation period, so Christ will come to take the church to live with Him at the end of His period of separation from the church (John 14:3).

Just as the taking of the Jewish bride was accomplished by a procession of the bridegroom and male escorts from the bridegroom's father's house to the home of the bride, so the taking of the church will be accomplished by a procession of Christ and an angelic escort from Christ's Father's house in heaven to the home of the church (1 Thessalonians 4:16).

Analogous with the Jewish bride not knowing the exact time of the bridegroom's arrival, the church does not know the exact time of Christ's coming for her.

In the same way that the Jewish bridegroom's arrival was preceded by a shout, so Christ's arrival to take the church will be preceded by a shout (1 Thessalonians 4:16).

Similar to the Jewish bride's return with the bridegroom to his father's house after her departure from her home, the church will return with Christ to His Father's house in heaven after she is snatched from the earth to meet Him in the air (1 Thessalonians 4:17; John 14:2-3).

In the same manner as the Jewish wedding party found wedding guests assembled in the bridegroom's father's house when they arrived, so Christ and the church will find the souls of Old Testament saints assembled in heaven when they arrive. These souls will serve as the wedding guests.

Parallel to the custom of the Jewish bridegroom and bride entering into physical union after their arrival at the bridegroom's father's house, thereby consummating the marriage that had been covenanted earlier, Christ and the church will experience spiritual union after their arrival at His Father's house in heaven, thereby consummating their relationship that had been covenanted earlier.

As the Jewish bride remained hidden in the bridal chamber for seven days after arrival at the bridegroom's father's house, the church will remain hidden for a period of seven years after arrival at Christ's Father's house in heaven. While the seven-year Tribulation Period is occurring on the earth, the church will be in heaven, totally hidden from the sight of those living on the earth.

Just as the Jewish bridegroom brought his bride out of the bridal chamber at the end of the seven days with her veil removed so all could see his bride, so Christ will bring the church out of heaven in His Second Coming, after the seven-year Tribulation in full view of all who are alive, so all can see who the true church is (Colossians 3:4).

The Significance of the Analogy

This analogy between Jewish marriage customs and Christ's relationship to the church is beautiful. But you may be wondering what practical significance it has for today. First, if you have never taken Jesus Christ personally to be your Savior from sin, this analogy holds great significance for you. Christ came to this earth and died on a cross to pay the penalty for your sins. Through shedding His blood, He paid the price necessary to purchase you to be part of His Bride, the church. He thereby established a new covenant through which you can enter a special relationship with Him.

Every time the gospel of Jesus Christ is declared to you, Christ is proposing that you enter this special relationship with Him. In essence He is saying to you:

"I, Jesus, take thee, sinner, to be My Bride. And I do promise and covenant before God The Father and these witnesses, to be thy loving and faithful Savior and Bridegroom; in sickness and in health, in plenty and in want, in joy and in sorrow, in faithfulness and in waywardness, for time and for eternity."

Just as the bride could accept or reject the Jewish bridegroom's proposal, so you can accept or reject Christ's proposal to you. If you reject it throughout this lifetime, then you never will be rightly related to Jesus Christ. As a tragic result, you will spend eternity separated from God and Christ in the eternal lake of fire.

If, however, you accept Christ's proposal, your sins will be forgiven, and you will enter that relationship that makes you part of His Bride, the church. Additionally, you will go to be with Him when He comes to take the church, and you will remain with Him forever in great blessing.

Accepting Christ's proposal is quite simple. If you sincerely believe that Jesus Christ is the Son of God and that He came to this earth, died for your sins, and rose from the dead, then respond to Him as follows:

"I, sinner, take Thee, Jesus, to be my Savior. And I do promise and covenant before God and these witnesses to be Thy loving and faithful Bride; in sickness and in health, in plenty and in want, in joy and in sorrow, for time and for eternity."

Second, the analogy is most significant also for those who have taken Christ to be their Savior. During the time of separation between the establishment of the marriage covenant and the coming of the bridegroom to take his bride, the Jewish bride could have committed adultery by giving herself to another man. In like manner, it is possible for believers today to commit spiritual adultery against Christ before He returns to take His church. Paul expressed concern over this possibility when he wrote the following to Christians:

"For I am jealous over you with godly jealousy: for I have espoused you to one husband, that I may present you as a chaste virgin to Christ. But I fear lest by any means, as the serpent beguiled Eve through his craftiness, so your minds should be corrupted from the simplicity that is in Christ" (2 Corinthians 11:2-3).

James expressed the same concern when he rebuked Christians: "Ye adulterers and adulteresses, know ye not that the friendship with the world is enmity with God? Whosoever, therefore, will be a friend of the world is the enemy of God" (James 4:4). The context of James' statement indicates that spiritual adultery is committed when a believer becomes more devoted to the godless world system and the things that please it than he is to Jesus Christ and the things that please Him.

If you are a believer, honestly evaluate your devotion to Jesus Christ. Do you love Him as much now as when you took Him to be your Savior? Is He truly the center of your existence, the One who gives your life its meaning and purpose? Is your every attitude, action, and lifestyle motivated and controlled by your devotion to Jesus Christ or by a desire to have the friendship of the world system in which you live?

If you have been unfaithful to your heavenly Bridegroom, confess this to Him and be assured that even if we are faithless, "yet he abideth faithful: he cannot deny himself" (2 Timothy 2:13). Then trust the Holy Spirit to renew your devotion as you wait for your heavenly Bridegroom to come at any moment.

Dr. Renald E. Showers is widely recognized as one of the most distinguished theologians in America today. A graduate of Philadelphia College of Bible (now Cairn University), he holds a B.A. in history from Wheaton College, a Th.M. in church history from Dallas Theological Seminary, and a Th.D. in theology from Grace Theological Seminary. He is an international conference speaker for The Friends of Israel Gospel Ministry, Inc., and a contributing editor for *Israel My Glory* magazine.

Appendix E

The following is a short play adapted from *Behold The Bridgroom Comes*, written by Dr. Renald Showers. The play is written by Terry Burnside.

Behold The Bridegroom Comes

Cast of Characters

Bridegroom:

Bride:

Bride's father:

Bridegroom's father:

Male Escorts: 1.   2.

Bridesmaids: 1.   2.

Friends and Guests:

1.   2.   3.

Best Man:

Bystanders:

1.   2.   3.

ACT 1

Groom: (thinking to himself and speaking out loud)
"My knees are knocking. My knees are knocking. I hope her father approves of my intention tonight. I've waited years for Mary. Now the time has come for me to ask for her hand in marriage. I'm already at the door of her house. I'll knock."

KNOCK

Bride's Father: (surprised and cautious)
"Joseph, Joseph, it's been months since we've spoken. How is your father Jacob?"

Groom: "He's well. He's well. I...I...would like to ask for the privilege of having Mary's hand in marriage."

Bride's Father: "Joseph, I couldn't be more pleased. I've watched you grow up. You've established yourself as an apprentice in your father's carpenter shop."

Groom: "I know now we need to negotiate a purchase price for Mary. I believe I could pay three hundred denarii."

Bride's Father: "Only three hundred, Joseph? Mary is beautiful, kind, and industrious. A wife for life surely is worth six hundred, but for you Joseph, my future son-in-law, four hundred."

Groom: "Agreed!"

Bride's Father: "Mary, come out. Mary, Joseph and I have agreed on your marriage and the price. Now pour a cup of wine and you two drink from it."

POUR WINE AND DRINK FROM THE SAME CUP

Bride's Father: "The marriage covenant has now united the two of you as husband and wife. Now you are married. Joseph, you know what to do in preparation to return for Mary."

Groom: "Mary, I'll come some day for you, my wife."

Bride: "I'll watch and wait for that day, for you Joseph, my beloved."

Groom: "Please excuse me Mary. I must go to my father's house now to prepare a place for you and then I will come again to receive you to myself. Good-bye Mary."

ACT 2

Groom: (talking to his best man, John, and other friends)

"John, tonight's the night. It's almost been a year. All preparations are now complete. I've been busily engaged in my father's house preparing for my wife and our lives together. Now, all that is left is to go to Mary's father's house and receive my bride."

Best Man: "It's time to light the torches for the procession to your bride's home. Let's leave Joseph. Your bride has kept herself for you."

JOSEPH, JOHN, AND FRIENDS LEAVE JOSEPH'S FATHER'S HOUSE

Bystanders: "Here comes the groom. Here comes the groom. See his wedding party? He's coming to claim his bride tonight."

SHOUTS BEGIN TO SOUND:
"BEHOLD, THE BRIDEGROOM COMES!
BEHOLD, THE BRIDEGROOM COMES!"

SHOUTS CONTINUE FROM STREET TO STREET UNTIL
ARRIVAL AT MARY'S FATHER'S HOUSE

Bride: (exclaims loudly)
"What's that I hear? Could it be my beloved coming for me tonight?
I'm, almost ready. I'll call my bridesmaids."

BRIDE STEPS OUT OF THE DOOR OF THE HOUSE

Bride: "Get over to my home as fast as you can. Get me dressed in
my bridal garment because tonight is the night. My groom is coming
to claim me. He will wait outside until I'm ready. But, hurry! Hurry!"

ACT 3

MARY LEAVES HER FATHER'S HOUSE

Bridegroom: "Mary, we will soon be united as one. I delight in you
and love you."

Bride: "I love you, my husband, my love."

Male Escorts: "Let's hurry to the father's house."

Bridesmaids: "Yes, let's hurry."

THE ENLARGED WEDDING PARTY HAS A RETURN TORCH-
LIGHT PROCESSION TO THE FATHER'S HOUSE

Father: "Welcome. Enter into joy."

Bridegroom: "The Banquet Hall is ready. The guests have arrived. We will join them soon. It's time to enter the Bridal Chamber, Mary. There we will consummate our union. Let's enter the *Huppah*."

BRIDEGROOM AND BRIDE ENTER THE HUPPAH TOGETHER AND THE BRIDEGROOM REENTERS THE BANQUET HALL AND MAKES AN ANNOUNCEMENT TO THE WEDDING PARTY

Bridegroom: "We have consummated our marriage. Rejoice in our joy and love. I'll keep my bride hidden from view for seven days. It's been our custom, these days of hiding, for many years. It's the days of the bridal chamber!"

FRIENDS AND GUESTS: (cheer)

"JOY IS YOURS! MAY THE LORD GOD BLESS! HAPPINESS FOREVER! JEHOVAH BE PRAISED!"

"Let's celebrate with a grand and glorious feast for seven days. PRAISE JEHOVAH!"

SEVEN DAYS PASS AND THE BRIDE REENTERS THE BANQUET HALL

Bridegroom: "Here is my Bride. Her veil is removed. Rejoice in her beauty and my love for her for all eternity."

THE END

Appendix F

Salvation and the Cross—God's Remedy and Man's Hope

The songwriter, Isaac Watts, penned it well, "At the cross, at the cross where I first saw the light, And the burden of my heart rolled away, It was there by faith I received my sight, And now I am happy all the day." Another composer, William R. Newell, gave us, "Years I spent in vanity and pride, Caring not my Lord was crucified, Knowing not it was for me He died On Calvary."

Are you singing in your heart? The hymns, *At Calvary* and *At the Cross,* contain so much truth about what God did for our salvation by sending His one and only Son to die on Calvary. It is God's plan from beginning to end. Salvation is found in only one person, Jesus Christ. He is God's remedy and man's only hope.

Jesus made a bold declaration in John 14:6, "Jesus answered, 'I am the way and the truth and the life. No one comes to the Father except through me.'" When Jesus said that, He was either a liar, a lunatic, or the Lord. For someone to claim He was the only way to Heaven when it was not true would make Him a deceiver indeed. To make this statement with no credentials would make Him a madman. But, to speak the truth of God and know He had come from the Father and was going back to the Father makes Him Lord.

Jesus is Savior—He died on the cross for our eternal redemption. This is called the atoning work of Christ. Atonement is the effect of Jesus' sufferings and death in redeeming mankind and bringing about the reconciliation of God to man. Christ's death paid God's penalty for our sin in order that those who believe might gain forgiveness and eternal life. God's penalty for sin is physical, spiritual, and eternal death. God's remedy, even though we may die physically, is that He has provided His Son to reconcile us to God and be saved from spiritual death. Then we no longer have to fear eternal death or the second death spoken of in the Book of Revelation.

Man has hope. We have hope. The world has hope. Hope is realized at the Cross. This is salvation. Do you know for certain that if you died today, you would go to Heaven? Jesus is the answer, remedy, and your only hope.

Terry Burnside

This article was written in 2006 when Central Church in Collierville, Tennessee studied the *40 Days of Faith: Discovering the Uniqueness of Christianity*, written by the leadership of Central Church, both Elders and the Senior Team. There were forty articles. I had the privilege of writing three of these articles.

Appendix G

The Return of Christ—Man's Greatest Expectation

Christ's return has been the expectation of believers since the birth of the Church on the Day of Pentecost. Paul would write Titus, "while we wait for the blessed hope—the appearing of the glory of our great God and Savior, Jesus Christ" (Titus 2:13).

Man's great expectation is wrapped with the hope of salvation, everlasting life, and the return of Jesus Christ to receive us to Himself. Christ has gone to prepare a place for us in His Father's House. He said He would come again to receive us to Himself and wherever He is, we will be also (John 14). Isn't this exciting! Our hope of the glorious appearing of our great God and Savior Jesus Christ should stir our souls. It is a comforting, purifying, and activating hope.

Paul told the church of Thessalonica that the coming of Jesus Christ would be like this: He will return from Heaven with a shout. He will cause the dead in Christ to rise first. He will implement the Rapture of the living saints as they are caught up together to meet Him in the air. What a moment of triumph, when both the resurrection of the Christian dead and raptured living saints, take place! All of us who know Jesus Christ as Savior and Lord will be part of that defining moment in time. We all will realize the Lord's presence in a way never known before as we meet Him in the air. Christ's promise to us is residence with Him forever.

No wonder Paul would say, "Therefore encourage one another with these words" (1 Thessalonians 4:18). Our blessed hope is first comforting. What a word of encouragement! We all need words of encouragement. We need words that bring healing. We need words that are full of mercy. Our God is the God of all comfort and all mercies.

Our hope also is purifying. See 1 John 2:29 and 1 John 3:1-3. One day we will be like Jesus Christ when He is revealed from Heaven. We shall see Him as He is. If you have this hope in you, you purify yourself, just as Jesus is pure. Let's just do it!

Got Jesus?

Finally, it is an activating hope. We are to do business and be in service for the King of kings and Lord of lords (Luke 19:13).

Whom are you expecting? His name is Jesus!

Rev. Terry Burnside

This article was written in 2006 when Central Church in Collierville, Tennessee studied the *40 Days of Faith: Discovering the Uniqueness of Christianity*, written by the leadership of Central Church, both Elders and the Senior Team. There were forty articles. I had the privilege of writing three of these articles.

Appendix H

Spiritual Gifts, Rewards, and Judgment:

I. The rewards associated with The Great Testing/The Judgment Seat of Christ (Bema)
(Luke 14:12-14; 1 Corinthians 3:10-15; Romans 14:9-12; 2 Corinthians 5:6-10)
All Christians will be judged, and the judgment will be based on works.

II. Five Crowns in the New Testament:

A. *Incorruptible or Imperishable Crown*
Crown given to victors who have obtained mastery over the old man (the old heart, mind, and will), the sinful self.

B. *Rejoicing or Soul Winner's Crown*
Crown for those who witness and win souls for Jesus Christ.

C. *Life or Martyr's Crown*
Crown for those who endure trials and are faithful unto death.

D. *Righteousness Crown or Rapture Crown*
Crown for those who are loving His appearing (ready and waiting) and are eagerly looking forward to Christ coming back again.
(That's me, Terry Burnside; is that you?)

E. *Glory or Service Crown*

Crown for those being willing to feed the flock of God.

III. Crowns

    A. May be won or lost (Revelation 3:10-11; 22:12).
       So that no one will take your crown; a call to perseverance.

    B. They are prizes (1 Corinthians 9:24; Philippians 3:13-14).

    C. Described as crowns of gold (Revelation 4:4, 10).

IV. What are rewards?

    A. Our capacity to enjoy God.

    B. Our responsibility for service.

    C. Our bottom line is to bring glory to God.

V. Even with spiritual gifts we still have trials.

    A. Crown of Life (James 1:1-4, 12; Revelation 2:8-11).

    B. Trials come to test our faith; we will be crowned with eternal life rich in rewards for faithfulness (1 Corinthians 4:1-2).

    C. Trials come to develop patience, steadfastness, endurance, and staying power (2 Corinthians 4:16-18; Romans 8:18; Matthew 11:28-30).

    D. Trials come to bring us to Christian maturity; goal of Christlikeness (Hebrews 5:11-14).

Appendix I

"Peace In The Middle East" — Senate Floor Statement By U.S.
Senator James M. Inhofe (R-OK)
March 4, 2002

I was interested the other day when I heard that the de facto ruler, Saudi Arabian Crown Prince Abdullah, made a statement which was received by many in this country as if it were a statement of fact, as if it were something new, a concept for peace in the Middle East that no one had ever heard of before. I was kind of shocked that it was so well received by many people who had been down this road before. I suggest to you that what Crown Prince Abdullah talked about a few days ago was not new at all. He talked about the fact that under the Abdullah plan, Arabs would normalize relations with Israel in exchange for the Jewish state surrendering the territory it received after the 1967 Six-Day War as if that were something new. He went on to talk about other land that had been acquired and had been taken by Israel. I remember so well on December 4 when we covered all of this and the fact that there isn't anything new about the prospect of giving up land that is rightfully Israel's land in order to have peace. When it gets right down to it, the land doesn't make that much difference because Yasser Arafat and others don't recognize Israel's right to any of the land. They do not recognize Israel's right to exist. I will discuss seven reasons, which I mentioned once before, why Israel is entitled to the land they have and that it should not be a part of the peace process. If this is something that Israel wants to do, it is their business to do it. But anyone who has tried to put the pressure on Israel to do this is wrong. We are going to be hit by skeptics who are going to say we will be attacked because of our support for Israel, and if we get out of the Middle East—that is us—all the problems will go away. That is just not true. If we withdraw, all of these problems will again come to our door. I have some observations to make about that. But I would like to reemphasize once again the seven reasons that Israel has the right to their land.

The first reason is that Israel has the right to the land because of all of the archeological evidence. That is reason, No. 1. All the archeological evidence supports it. Every time there is a dig in Israel, it does nothing but support the fact that Israelis have had a presence there for 3,000 years. They have been there for a long time. The coins, the cities, the pottery, the culture—there are other people, groups that are there, but there is no mistaking the fact that Israelis have been present in that land for 3,000 years. It predates any claims that other peoples in the regions may have. The ancient Philistines are extinct. Many other ancient peoples are extinct. They do not have the unbroken line to this date that the Israelis have. Even the Egyptians of today are not racial Egyptians of 2,000, 3,000 years ago. They are primarily an Arab people. The land is called Egypt, but they are not the same racial and ethnic stock as the old Egyptians of the ancient world. The first Israelis are in fact descended from the original Israelites. The first proof, then, is the archeology.

The second proof of Israel's right to the land is the historic right. History supports it totally and completely. We know there has been an Israel up until the time of the Roman Empire. The Romans conquered the land. Israel had no homeland, although Jews were allowed to live there. They were driven from the land in two dispersions: One was in 70 A.D. and the other was in 135 A.D. But there was always a Jewish presence in the land. The Turks, who took over about 700 years ago and ruled the land up until about World War I, had control. Then the land was conquered by the British. The Turks entered World War I on the side of Germany. The British knew they had to do something to punish Turkey, and also to break up that empire that was going to be a part of the whole effort of Germany in World War I. So the British sent troops against the Turks in the Holy Land. One of the generals who was leading the British armies was a man named Allenby. Allenby was a Bible-believing Christian. He carried a Bible with him everywhere he went and he knew the significance of Jerusalem. The night before the attack against Jerusalem to drive out the Turks, Allenby prayed that God would allow him to capture the city without doing damage to the holy places. That day, Allenby sent World War I biplanes over the city of Jerusalem to do a reconnaissance mission. You have to understand that the Turks had at that time never seen an airplane. So there they were, flying around. They looked in the sky and saw these fascinating inventions and did not know what they were, and they were terrified by them. Then they were told they were going to be opposed by a man named Allenby the next day, which means, in their language, "man sent from God" or "prophet from God." They dared not fight against a prophet from God, so the next morning, when Allenby went to take Jerusalem, he went in and captured it without firing a single shot.

The British Government was grateful to Jewish people around the world, particularly to one Jewish chemist who helped them manufacture niter. Niter is an ingredient that was used in nitroglycerin which was sent over from the New World. But they did not have a way of getting it to England. The German U-boats were shooting on the boats, so most of the niter they were trying to import to make nitroglycerin was at the bottom of the ocean. But a man named Weitzman, a Jewish chemist, discovered a way to make it from materials that existed in England. As a result, they were able to continue that supply. The British at that time said they were going to give the Jewish people a homeland. That is all a part of history. It is all written down in history. They were gratified that the Jewish people, the bankers, came through and helped finance the war. The homeland that Britain said it would set aside consisted of all of what is now Israel and all of what was then the nation of Jordan—the whole thing. That was what Britain promised to give the Jews in 1917. In the beginning, there was some Arab support for this action. There was not a huge Arab population in the land at that time, and there is a reason for that. The land was not able to sustain a large population of people. It just did not have the development it needed to handle those people, and the land was not really wanted by anybody. Nobody really wanted this land. It was considered to be worthless land. I want the Presiding Officer to hear what Mark Twain said. And, of course, you may have read "Huckleberry Finn" and "Tom Sawyer." Mark Twain—Samuel Clemens—took a tour of Palestine in 1867. This is how he described that land. We are talking about Israel now. He said: "A desolate country whose soil is rich enough but is given over wholly to weeds. A silent, mournful expanse. We never saw a human being on the whole route. There was hardly a tree or a shrub anywhere. Even the olive and the cactus, those fast friends of a worthless soil, had almost deserted the country." Where was this great Palestinian nation? It did not exist. It was not there. Palestinians were not there. Palestine was a region named by the Romans, but at that time it was under the control of Turkey, and there was no large mass of people there because the land would not support them.

This is the report that the Palestinian Royal Commission, created by the British, made. It quotes an account of the conditions on the coastal plain along the Mediterranean Sea in 1913. This is the Palestinian Royal Commission. They said: "The road leading from Gaza to the north was only a summer track, suitable for transport by camels or carts. No orange groves, orchards or vineyards were to be seen until one reached the Yavnev village. Houses were mud. Schools did not exist. The western part toward the sea was almost a desert. The villages in this area were few and thinly populated. Many villages were deserted by their inhabitants." That was 1913.

The French author Voltaire described Palestine as "a hopeless, dreary place." In short, under the Turks the land suffered from neglect and low population. That is a historic fact. The nation became populated by both Jews and Arabs because the land came to prosper when Jews came back and began to reclaim it. Historically, they began to reclaim it. If there had never been any archaeological evidence to support the rights of the Israelis to the territory, it is also important to recognize that other nations in the area have no longstanding claim to the country either. Did you know that Saudi Arabia was not created until 1913, Lebanon until 1920? Iraq did not exist as a nation until 1932, Syria until 1941; the borders of Jordan were established in 1946 and Kuwait in 1961. Any of these nations that would say Israel is only a recent arrival would have to deny their own rights as recent arrivals as well. They did not exist as countries. They were all under the control of the Turks.

Historically, Israel gained its independence in 1948. The third reason that land belongs to Israel is the practical value of the Israelis being there. Israel today is a modern marvel of agriculture. Israel is able to bring more food out of a desert environment than any other country in the world. The Arab nations ought to make Israel their friend and import technology from Israel that would allow all the Middle East, not just Israel, to become an exporter of food. Israel has unarguable success in its agriculture.

The fourth reason I believe Israel has the right to the land is on the grounds of humanitarian concern. You see, there were 6 million Jews slaughtered in Europe in World War II. The persecution against the Jews had been very strong in Russia since the advent of communism. It was against them even before then under the Czars. These people have a right to their homeland. If we are not going to allow them a homeland in the Middle East, then where? What other nation on Earth is going to cede territory, is going to give up land? They are not asking for a great deal. The whole nation of Israel would fit into my home State of Oklahoma seven times. It would fit into the Presiding Officer's State of Georgia seven times. They are not asking for a great deal. The whole nation of Israel is very small. It is a nation that, up until the time that claims started coming in, was not desired by anybody.

The fifth reason Israel ought to have their land is that she is a strategic ally of the United States. Whether we realize it or not, Israel is a detriment, an impediment, to certain groups hostile to democracies and hostile to what we believe in, hostile to that which makes us the greatest nation in the history of the world. They have kept them from taking complete control of the Middle East. If it were not for Israel, they would overrun the region. They are our strategic ally. It is good to know we have a friend in the Middle East on whom we can count. They vote with us in the United Nations more than England, more than Canada, more than France, more than Germany—more than any other country in the world.

The sixth reason is that Israel is a roadblock to terrorism. The war we are now facing is not against a sovereign nation; it is against a group of terrorists who are very fluid, moving from one country to another. They are almost invisible. That is whom we are fighting against today. We need every ally we can get. If we do not stop terrorism in the Middle East, it will be on our shores. We have said this again and again and again, and it is true. One of the reasons I believe the spiritual door was opened for an attack against the United States of America is that the policy of our Government has been to ask the Israelis, and demand it with pressure, not to retaliate in a significant way against the terrorist strikes that have been launched against them. Since its independence in 1948, Israel has fought four wars: The war in 1948 and 1949—that was the war for independence—the war in 1956, the Sinai campaign; the Six-Day War in 1967; and in 1973, the Yom Kippur War, the holiest day of the year, and that was with Egypt and Syria. You have to understand that in all four cases, Israel was attacked. They were not the aggressor. Some people may argue that this was not true because they went in first in 1956, but they knew at that time that Egypt was building a huge military to become the aggressor. Israel, in fact, was not the aggressor and has not been the aggressor in any of the four wars. Also, they won all four wars against impossible odds. They are great warriors. They consider a level playing field being outnumbered 2 to 1. There were 39 Scud missiles that landed on Israeli soil during the gulf war. Our President asked Israel not to respond. In order to have the Arab nations on board, we asked Israel not to participate in the war. They showed tremendous restraint and did not. Now we have asked them to stand back and not do anything over these last several attacks. We have criticized them. We have criticized them in our media. Local people in television and radio often criticize Israel, not knowing the true facts. We need to be informed. I was so thrilled when I heard a reporter pose a question to our Secretary of State, Colin Powell. He said: Mr. Powell, the United States has advocated a policy of restraint in the Middle East. We have discouraged Israel from retaliation again and again and again because we've said it leads to continued escalation—that it escalates the violence. Are we going to follow that preaching ourselves? Mr. Powell indicated we would strike back. In other words, we can tell Israel not to do it, but when it hits us, we are going to do something.

But all that changed in December when the Israelis went into the Gaza with gunships and into the West Bank with F-16s. With the exception of last May, the Israelis had not used F-16s since the 1967 6-Day War. And I am so proud of them because we have to stop terrorism. It is not going to go away. If Israel were driven into the sea tomorrow, if every Jew in the Middle East were killed, terrorism would not end. You know that in your heart. Terrorism would continue. It is not just a matter of Israel in the Middle East. It is the heart of the very people who are perpetrating this stuff. Should they be successful in overrunning Israel—which they won't be—but should they be, it would not be enough. They will never be satisfied.

No. 7, I believe very strongly that we ought to support Israel; that it has a right to the land. This is the most important reason: Because God said so. As I said a minute ago, look it up in the book of Genesis. It is right up there on the desk. In Genesis 13:14-17, the Bible says: "The Lord said to Abram, 'Lift up now your eyes, and look from the place where you are northward, and southward, and eastward and westward: for all the land which you see, to you will I give it, and to your seed forever. Arise, walk through the land in the length of it and in the breadth of it; for I will give it to thee.'" That is God talking. The Bible says that Abram removed his tent and came and dwelt in the plain of Mamre, which is in Hebron, and built there an altar before the Lord. Hebron is in the West Bank. It is at this place where God appeared to Abram and said, "I am giving you this land,"—the West Bank. This is not a political battle at all. It is a contest over whether or not the Word of God is true.

The seven reasons, I am convinced, clearly establish that Israel has a right to the land. Eight years ago on the lawn of the White House, Yitzhak Rabin shook hands with PLO Chairman Yasser Arafat. It was an historic occasion. It was a tragic occasion. At that time, the official policy of the Government of Israel began to be, "Let us appease the terrorists. Let us begin to trade the land for peace." This process continued unabated up until last year. Here in our own Nation, at Camp David, in the summer of 2000, then Prime Minister of Israel Ehud Barak offered the most generous concessions to Yasser Arafat that had ever been laid on the table. He offered him more than 90 percent of all the West Bank territory, sovereign control of it. There were some parts he did not want to offer, but in exchange for that he said he would give up land in Israel proper that the PLO had not even asked for. And he also did the unthinkable. He even spoke of dividing Jerusalem and allowing the Palestinians to have their capital there in the East. Yasser Arafat stormed out of the meeting. Why did he storm out of the meeting? Everything he had said he wanted was offered there. It was put into his hands. Why did he storm out of the meeting?

A couple of months later, there began to be riots, terrorism. The riots began when now Prime Minister Ariel Sharon went to the Temple Mount. And this was used as the thing that lit the fire and that caused the explosion. Did you know that Sharon did not go unannounced and that he contacted the Islamic authorities before he went and secured their permission and had permission to be there? It was no surprise. The response was very carefully calculated. They knew the world would not pay attention to the details. They would portray this in the Arab world as an attack upon the holy mosque. They would portray it as an attack upon that mosque and use it as an excuse to riot. Over the last eight years, during this time of the peace process, where the Israeli public has pressured its leaders to give up land for peace because they are tired of fighting, there has been increased terror. In fact, it has been greater in the last eight years than any other time in Israel's history. Showing restraint and giving in has not produced any kind of peace. It is so much so that today the leftist peace movement in Israel does not exist because the people feel they were deceived. They did offer a hand of peace, and it was not taken. That is why the politics of Israel have changed drastically over the past twelve months. The Israelis have come to see that, "No matter what we do, these people do not want to deal with us. They want to destroy us." That is why even yet today the stationery of the PLO still has upon it the map of the entire state of Israel, not just the tiny little part they call the West Bank that they want. They want it all. We have to get out of this mindset that somehow you can buy peace in the Middle East by giving little plots of land. It has not worked before when it has been offered. These seven reasons show why Israel is entitled to that land.

It is my understanding that since the speech was given on the Senate floor that it is part of the public domain. Please feel free to include in the appendix of your book.

Thanks,

Jacob T. Heisten—Press Secretary